Tara Forrest
Realism as Protest

**Film**

*For Christoph and Julian*

**Tara Forrest** lectures in Screen Studies at the University of Technology, Sydney. She is the author of »The Politics of Imagination: Benjamin, Kracauer, Kluge« (also published by transcript).

Tara Forrest
# Realism as Protest
**Kluge, Schlingensief, Haneke**

[transcript]

Research for this book was generously supported by
the Australian Research Council.

**Bibliographic Information published by the Deutsche Nationalbibliothek**
The Deutsche Nationalbibliothek lists this publication in the Deutsche Nationalbibliografie; detailed bibliographic data are available in the Internet at
http://dnb.d-nb.de

**© 2015 transcript Verlag, Bielefeld**

All rights reserved. No part of this book may be reprinted or reproduced or utilized in any form or by any electronic, mechanical, or other means, now known or hereafter invented, including photocopying and recording, or in any information storage or retrieval system, without permission in writing from the publisher.

Cover layout: Kordula Röckenhaus, Bielefeld
Cover illustration: Christoph Schlingensief, Quiz 3000 (2002).
  © Thomas Aurin.
Layout: Justine Haida
Printed and bound in Great Britain by Marston Book Services Ltd, Oxfordshire
Print-ISBN 978-3-8376-2973-6
PDF-ISBN 978-3-8394-2973-0

# Content

**Introduction** | 7

**CHAPTER 1**
Subjunctive Realism:
Kluge on Film, Politics, and Feelings | 11

**CHAPTER 2**
Creative Co-Productions:
Kluge's Television Experiments | 45

**CHAPTER 3**
Mobilising the Public Sphere:
Schlingensief's Reality Theatre | 69

**CHAPTER 4**
Productive Discord: Schlingensief, Adorno,
and *Freakstars 3000* | 95

**CHAPTER 5**
From Information to Experience:
Christoph Schlingensief's *Quiz 3000* | 117

**CHAPTER 6**
A Negative Utopia:
Michael Haneke's Fragmentary Cinema | 141

**References** | 169

# Introduction

> [A]rt no longer has the task of representing a reality that is preexisting for everyone in common, but rather of revealing, in its isolation, the very cracks that reality would like to cover over in order to exist in safety; and that, in doing so, it repels reality.
> 
> THEODOR W. ADORNO[1]

> The modern form of Fascistisation is much more the mass mobilisation of passivity, of collective inattention.
> 
> ALEXANDER KLUGE[2]

In the *Poetikvorlesungen* (Poetics Lectures) he delivered in Frankfurt in 2012, Alexander Kluge argues that the Frankfurt School tradition of Critical Theory "works with an antagonistic conception of realism". For Kluge, who is a contemporary heir to that tradition, reality is not a straightforward concept that accurately reflects the world in which we live. While "[t]his reality", he states, "is real in the sense [...] that an accident kills people, or that wars exist", it is also a

---

[1] | Theodor W. Adorno, "Why is the New Art so Hard to Understand?" in: Theodor W. Adorno, *Essays on Music*, Berkeley and Los Angeles: University of California Press, 2002, p.131.

[2] | Alexander Kluge, "Die Utopie Film (1983)" in: Alexander Kluge, *In Gefahr und größter Not bringt der Mittelweg den Tod. Texte zu Kino, Film, Politik*, ed. Christian Schulte, Berlin: Vorwerk 8, 1999, p. 94.

"cocoon" we build around ourselves in order to "keep reality out". As Kluge makes clear, the image of reality represented, for example, in the mainstream news media does not necessarily bear a meaningful relationship to the possibilities inherent in existing circumstances. "It is", he argues, "characterised by an extreme rigidity, a hardness. It sits in jail and bangs its head against the wall when it notice[s] how objective real relationships are".[3]

This violent, disaffected image of reality – embodied in the figure of someone locked in a cell banging their head against a wall – is an important one because it evokes a palpable sense of the degree to which it is both removed from the real conditions of the everyday world and mindful of its status as an ideological construction. As Kluge's description makes clear, this rigid conception of reality is seriously flawed because real conditions cannot be described in relation to an objective state that is removed from the subjective input of people who experience reality first hand. He argues, rather, that it is subjectivity embodied in the form of human experience that serves as a form of resistance to so called "objective" conceptions of reality.

If the productions explored in this book are driven by what Kluge describes as a "realism of protest" then it is because they cultivate a subjective mode of engagement that challenges the status quo. Although disparate in their form and content, each of the works can be described as "realistic", not because they accurately reflect a particular political or social reality, but because they encourage viewers to become active participants in the meaning-making process; to draw on their own capacity for experience in an attempt to make sense of the material in question. For Kluge "this capacity to make an effort, to strain something in oneself, to strain something in the senses"[4] is part and parcel of what it means to lead a vital and productive existence. When, he writes, someone "sits in front of the television watching *Deutschland sucht ein Superstar* on Saturday or in January

---

**3** | Alexander Kluge, *Theorie der Erzählung. Frankfurter Poetikvorlesungen*, 2013.

**4** | Ibid.

1939 listens to Radio Leipzig", then this capacity is not put into practice.[5]

As this statement suggests, there is a certain passivity cultivated by the rigid form of the constructed realities generated by the mainstream media; a rigidity that stymies the capacity to conceive of the extent to which reality could, in fact, be very different. As Christoph Schlingensief makes clear: "One sees an image and thinks that is the world, but forgets that there are actually many images of the world. That one also has within oneself many images, ideas, longings that couldn't be satisfied on which one continues to depend to the point where one could cry. Because one had to give them up. The human being consists not just of chemisty, but also of so much longing".[6]

As Kluge's delineation of reality banging its head against a wall suggests, reality – in the restrictive sense of the term – is deeply alienated from this longing because it is divorced from the subjective needs of the constituency it is supposed to represent. If the productions explored in this book cultivate feeling then it is not because they seek to channel the viewer's response in a particular direction, but because they cultivate a certain "obstinacy" (*Eigensinn*) in the face of existing circumstances; circumstances that lock people into accepting an image of reality that neither supports nor sustains their own interests.

Obstinacy, in this context, refers not only to a straightforward refusal of reality but to a mode of engagement that is driven not by the machinations of an external force but which is guided by one's "own sense" or "meaning" (*Eigensinn*). The productions explored in this book are significant not because they seek to close down meaning by presenting the viewer with a pre-packaged image of how reality *should* be, but because they actively cultivate this *Eigensinn* in the face of a dissatisfying reality; a reality that bangs its head against the

---

**5** | Ibid.
**6** | Christoph Schlingensief, *Christoph Schlingensief: Ich weiß, ich war's*, ed. Aino Laberenz, Köln: Kiepenheuer & Witsch, 2012, p. 52.

wall once it realises that so-called objective conditions are, in reality, not real. "We live", Kluge states, "in our subjectivity. That is our life. And that is obstinate".[7]

---

**7** | Alexander Kluge "Tür an Tür mit einem anderen Leben" (Radio Interview), *Das Blaue Sofa*, 2006.

# CHAPTER 1

Subjunctive Realism:

Kluge on Film, Politics, and Feelings

> We are surrounded by subjunctives, by the form of possibility. It could all be very different.
>
> ALEXANDER KLUGE[1]

Alexander Kluge's experimental film, television, and literary work is underpinned by a conception of realism that he describes as "subjunctive"[2] and "antagonistic"[3]. As Kluge makes clear, it is "antagonistic" because it is pitted against the pervasive idea that the reality in

---

[1] | Peter Laudenbach and Alexander Kluge,'"Träume sind die Nahrung auf dem Weg zum Ziel"', *brand eins: Wirtschaftsmagazin* 8, 2009, p. 26.

[2] | In addition to the reference above, see also Peter Laudenbach and Alexander Kluge, '"Wir sind Glückssucher"', *Der Tagesspiegel*, February 13, 2012: http://www.tagesspiegel.de/kultur/wir-sind-glueckssucher/6201290.html. Last accessed 1 November 2014.

[3] | See, for example, Alexander Kluge, "The Sharpest Ideology: That Reality Appeals to its Realistic Character" in: *Alexander Kluge: Raw Materials For the Imagination*, ed. Tara Forrest, Amsterdam: Amsterdam University Press, 2012, p. 192 and Heiner Boehncke and Alexander Kluge, "Die Rebellion des Stoffs gegen die Form und der Form gegen den Stoff: Der Protest als Erzähler" in: *Das B. Traven-Buch*, ed. Heiner Boehncke, Johannes Beck and Klaus Bergmann, Reinbek bei Hamburg: Rowohlt, 1976, p. 342. Kluge also discusses this concept in his lecture series: Alexander Kluge, *Theorie der Erzählung: Frankfurter Poetikvorlesungen*, Berlin: Suhrkamp, 2013.

which we live – as both experienced by people on an everyday basis and represented by the mainstream media – accurately reflects the myriad possibilities inherent in existing circumstances. Within this schema, the edict commonly espoused by politicians – that when reflecting on politics, policy, and the possibilities of the future one must, in fact, be *realistic* – is indebted to a conception of realism that is committed to the maintenance of the status quo. "Public opinion", Kluge argues, "is very strongly determined by people who [...] furnish themselves in reality as if in a tank or a knight's armour".[4] As this statement makes clear, this hegemonic conception of realism (of what it means to *be realistic*) is, for Kluge, extremely limiting, not only because it functions to protect the interests of those who employ it as both shield and weapon, but because it disregards the subjunctive realities that "exist side by side with reality"[5] that are borne out of the feelings and wishes of people who actually "want something completely different".[6] For Kluge, these subjunctive realities are significant because, as alternative visions of what *could* be, they play an important role in mobilising thought, discussion, and debate about how – and with what effects – the so-called reality in which we live could be transformed into something very different.

It is this capacity for interrogating reality – for actively imagining alternatives to the status quo – that, for Kluge, constitutes a truly realistic approach; an approach that is fueled by a dissatisfaction with, and a desire to protest against the prevailing conditions. "If", he writes, "I levy a protest against the reality principle, against that which this reality does to me, I am realistic".[7] It is thus not the real-

---

4 | Claus Phillip, "Vertrauenswürdige Irrtümer: Ein Gespräch mit Alexander Kluge", *Kolik*, 13 (2000), p. 10.
5 | Laudenbach, "'Wir sind Glückssucher'".
6 | Kluge, "The Sharpest Ideology: That Reality Appeals to its Realistic Character", p. 190.
7 | Alexander Kluge, "Interview von Ulrich Gregor (1976)" in: Alexander Kluge, *In Gefahr und größter Not bringt der Mittelweg den Tod: Texte zu Kino, Film, Politik*, ed. Christian Schulte, Berlin: Vorwerk 8, 1999, p. 229.

ity principle but "the realism of the human brain with its reshaping reaction to reality" that is "the fundamental condition of realism".[8]

This "reshaping" capacity (which Kluge describes as "the species given nature of protest"[9]) has, however, been stifled by the emphasis placed by politicians and the mainstream news media on the importance of being "realistic"; of channeling one's energies and confining one's hopes to activities and goals that are recognized by and sit comfortably within the paradigm supporting and maintaining the status quo. Within this schema, Kluge argues that "reality" (in this restrictive sense) is not a "natural state" that exists autonomously outside the subject.[10] On the contrary, he argues that it is manifested in a mode of thinking that has been imposed on the subject via ideology; an ideology so pervasive that it has overridden the instinctive capacity – inherent in our feelings – for distinguishing not only between right and wrong, but between that which works for or against our own interests. Extending the metaphors described above, the reality-principle functions, in this context, as a tank or suit of armour that inhibits feeling because it seals the subject off and anaesthetises him/her from the capacity to make connections and draw distinctions that are grounded in the experiences of the subject.

In what follows, I will analyse the degree to which the realistic method underpinning the experimental form of Kluge's films is driven by a desire to "motivate feelings"[11]; to break through the ideological straight jacket imposed by the reality-principle in an attempt to facilitate thinking, discussion, and debate about the possibilities for cultural and political change. Focusing on two films – *The Patriot* (*Die Patriotin*) (1979) and *War and Peace* (*Krieg und Frieden*) (1982) – that were directed and co-directed by Kluge respectively, this chap-

---

**8** | Kluge, "The Sharpest Ideology: That Reality Appeals to its Realistic Character", p. 193.
**9** | Ibid.
**10** | Kluge, "Interview von Ulrich Gregor (1976)", p. 229.
**11** | Alexander Kluge, *Die Macht der Gefühle*, Frankfurt am Main: Zweitausendeins, 1984, p. 212.

ter will explore how and with what effects Kluge has sought to mobilize debate about what he describes as the "porosity" of the present.[12]

## THE ANTI-REALISM OF FEELINGS

The significant role that feelings can play as bellwethers of a desire for change is integrally bound with Kluge's delineation of the task of a realistic method. For Kluge, feelings are significant because they are endowed with the capacity to "make distinctions". "It is", he notes, "constitutive of human beings and our species that we can distinguish between hot and cold, between what attracts me and what repels me, between what we will gladly watch and what we cannot bear to see".[13] This natural capacity is instinctive.[14] It is not borne of logic or the intellect. Rather, it is an ability which is grounded in the senses and which enables us to gain and consolidate experience that, in turn, guides and informs our decisions. Feelings, Kluge claims, are "happiness seekers"[15] and it is this capacity to both make and act

---

12 | Stuart Liebman, "On New German Cinema, Art, Enlightenment, and the Public Sphere: An Interview with Alexander Kluge," *October*, 46 (Fall, 1988), p. 38.

13 | Florian Hopf, "'Feelings Can Move Mountains...': An Interview with Alexander Kluge on the Film *The Power of Feelings*" in: *Alexander Kluge: Raw Materials for the Imagination*, ed. Tara Forrest, p. 243. Kluge elaborates on this capacity in Rainer Stollmann, "Nicht Alles, was einen in Wallung bringt, ist ein Gefühl: Gespräch mit Alexander Kluge" in: *Die Frage des Zusammenhangs: Alexander Kluge im Kontext*, ed. Christian Schulte, Berlin: Verlag Vorwerk 8, 2012, pp. 183-185.

14 | "Let's just say", Kluge notes, "that we have inherited a lot. We've even been endowed with instinctive functions that rumble away under the surface, in the so-called reptilian brain". Hopf, "'Feelings Can Move Mountains...'", p. 241.

15 | Alexander Kluge, "Text der Pressekonferenz mit Alexander Kluge über *Die Macht der Gefühle* in Venedig am 5. September 1983", *Kinemathek*, 20 (September, 1983), p. 5.

on distinctions that is a constitutive element of what it means to lead a vital and productive existence.¹⁶

However, as Kluge makes clear, this vital capacity has – over time – been significantly diminished. "I have the impression", he states,

> that, at some stage in the twelfth century, the feelings were massively suppressed in our country, banished with witch trials and terror into an intimate sphere where they're just not talked about. It may be the case that, historically speaking, this happened at a different time; at any rate, the feelings were *disempowered*. It's almost as if a decree went out that, while women and children may have feelings, the important men's business is to be dealt with realistically, through the intellect, or rather, through the false application of the intellect.¹⁷

As Kluge makes clear, the guiding assumption of the reality-principle – that when making plans and forming decisions one must *be realistic* – is bolstered by a system of reasoning that is completely divorced from the knowledge of the senses. "The whole culture industry", he states, "is busy persuading people to divide their senses and their consciousness"; to not "interest themselves in the elementary basis of their awareness, in their way of observing, in their sensuality."¹⁸ For Kluge, this split has profound implications for how people relate to and participate in the political sphere because – alienated from the capacity to draw distinctions based on their own experiences, feelings, and wishes – the responsibility for determining what is and isn't possible, what is a desirable reality and what isn't, is delegated to external authorities that harness feelings in aid of their own interests.

---

16 | Jochen Rack, "Gespräch mit Alexander Kluge: Wir Leben doch nicht nur in einer Gegenwart", *Sinn und Form*, 60.4 (2008), p. 481.
17 | Florian Hopf, '"Feelings Can Move Mountains..."', p. 244.
18 | Jan Dawson, '"But Why are the Questions so Abstract?': An Interview with Alexander Kluge" in: *Alexander Kluge and the Occasional Work of a Female Slave*, ed. Jan Dawson, New York: Zoetrope, 1977, p. 37.

Within this schema, Kluge argues that feelings become "traitors" because, instead of protecting the best interests of the subject, they are deployed (in aid, for example, of "patriotism" and "industrial discipline") as a form of "putty that holds everything together", even when the logic driving and maintaining the status quo works directly against their own interests.[19] Summarizing this situation, Kluge argues that feelings can be likened to "proletarians who find themselves confronted with the choice between unemployment and accepting nuclear power plants". "Now", he adds, "they are even standing up for rationalization and denouncing trouble-makers" because they have resigned themselves to the status quo out of a position of self-defence.[20]

As this example makes clear, the elemental capacity of feelings to draw distinctions based on both instinct and experience has, in this context, been overridden by a form of logic that complicates and undermines the subject's ability to make and act on decisions based on their sense of how things *should* be. "The intellect", Kluge states, "has concluded a pact with dietetics. How you feed yourself, how you earn a living, how you adapt to power, out of self-defence. The intellect has learned the art of self-defence. No one thinks except out of necessity."[21]

This split – between the intellect and a form of experience which is grounded in the knowledge of the senses – is a divide which, for Kluge, must be overcome if feelings are to "exert a practical critique"[22] of the restrictive and repressive logic underpinning the reality principle. Although "present in all countries", he argues that this

---

**19** | Florian Hopf, '"Feelings Can Move Mountains..."', pp. 243-4. "Feelings", in this context, are "used as motives (driving forces), and against our better knowledge at that: 'I'm feeling uneasy about this, but you just have to keep going, don't you?'", p. 245.

**20** | Ibid., pp. 245-6.

**21** | Ibid., p. 245.

**22** | Alexander Kluge and Klaus Eder, "Debate on the Documentary Film: Conversation with Klaus Eder, 1980" in: *Alexander Kluge: Raw Materials For the Imagination*, p. 198.

disjunction (between the intellect and experience, between the "specialized area" of politics and the "intensity of [...] everyday feeling") has, in Germany, functioned as a catalyst for a series of activities, decisions and events that have led to catastrophic outcomes. Extrapolating on these ideas in relation to the Holocaust, Kluge argues that:

it is thoroughly unpractical if the emotional shock of German families, which would have meant something important for the victims of Auschwitz in 1942, is made up for in 1979; for today it is an essentially useless, that is, timeless form of shock. The fact that we in our country are always shocked at the wrong moments and are not shocked at the right ones – and I am now talking about something very bad – is a consequence of our considering politics as a specialised area which others look after for us and not as a degree of intensity of our own feelings.²³

Central to Kluge's conception of the task of a realistic method is the degree to which an experimental film practice can reactivate the senses, sharpen perception and, in the process, reconnect the viewer with the political sphere. Politics, in this sense, is transformed from a professional, logic governed domain populated by strategists, experts, and politicians into a mode of perception that is characterised by a *"particular degree of intensity* of everything and everybody, of everyday feeling".²⁴ For Kluge, this transformation is significant because he argues that "direct perception has a capacity for self-regulation that logic doesn't have. With logic [which he elsewhere describes as the product of an "anchorless intellect"²⁵] I can just as well be a guard at

---

23 | Alexander Kluge, "The Political as Intensity of Everyday Feelings" in: *Alexander Kluge: Raw Materials For the Imagination*, p. 288.
24 | Ibid.
25 | "An anchorless intellect", he states, "is no use to anyone, and it can make one inhuman". See Angelika Wittlich, *Alle Gefühle glauben an einer glücklichen Ausgang*, 2002. The film is available in Alexander Kluge, *Die poetische Kraft der Theorie & Alle Gefühle glauben an einen glücklichen Ausgang*, Vol. 34, Edition Filmmuseum (2009).

a concentration camp as I can be a chief strategist at the Pentagon. But my diaphragm won't lead me there. My eyes and my ears won't lead me there."[26] This is because the instinctive function of feelings – which can distinguish intuitively between something which is fair and unjust, between that which is disturbing and pleasing – has the capacity to protest against a form of reality that generates fear, unhappiness, and suffering. Kluge describes this elementary, albeit undervalued capacity as the "anti-realism of feelings"[27] – a capacity he seeks to reignite via the experimental form of his films.

## THE FILM IN THE SPECTATOR'S HEAD

The realistic method driving the construction of Kluge's work is based on a conception of "realism that takes the imagination and wishes of human beings just as seriously as the world of facts."[28] A "materialist" film practice, he argues, does not seek to impose its ideas on the audience but rather encourages the viewer to draw on their own experience and imagination in order to participate autonomously in the meaning-making process. As Kluge makes clear: "We call this position materialist because it thinks from the bottom up, from the spectator and the cinema in his mind, to the cinema on screen".[29] Meaning, in this sense, is not conveyed directly by, nor contained autonomously within the film itself. Rather, it is generated by a process of exchange between the audience and the film that is initiated but not foreclosed by the director. Such a film practice seeks neither to explain nor generate understanding. "Understand-

---

26 | Alexander Kluge, "Interview von Ulrich Gregor (1976)", p. 242-3.
27 | See, for example, Peter Laudenbach,'"Träume sind die Nahrung auf dem Weg zum Ziel"', p. 2 and Alexander Kluge, "Ein Hauptansatz des Ulmer Instituts (1980)", in Kluge, *In Gefahr und größter Not bringt der Mittelweg den Tod*, ed. Christian Schulte, p. 59.
28 | Kluge, "Ein Hauptansatz des Ulmer Instituts (1980)", p. 59
29 | Jan Dawson, "'But Why are the Questions so Abstract?'", pp. 33-4.

ing a film is", Kluge writes, "conceptual imperialism which colonizes its objects. If I have understood everything then something has been emptied out. We must make films that thoroughly oppose such imperialism of consciousness".[30]

According to Kluge, both Hollywood cinema and conventional documentary film are incongruous with this materialist model. What troubles him about the former is the "strict separation" that exists between films that are organised around generating entertainment and the experiences of the viewers who are watching them.[31] "Excite the viewer, but there can't be any consequences" is, he notes, one of the "guiding principle[s] of the entertainment industry in Hollywood".[32] Instead of taking the audience seriously as "co-producers", Kluge argues that Hollywood films encourage "the audience to give up their own experience and follow the more organised experience of the film".[33] Instead of relying on and/or cultivating the viewer's own capacity to draw distinctions, the refined form of Hollywood films channels the viewer's feelings in specific directions, leaving the audience with scant opportunity to reflect on and/or think autonomously about the issues and ideas at hand. "*Öffentlichkeit* [a public sphere] without *Erfahrung* [experience]", Kluge states, "[t]hat is the cinema today".[34]

---

**30** | Alexander Kluge, "On Film and the Public Sphere" in: *Alexander Kluge: Raw Materials For the Imagination*, p. 38.
**31** | Stuart Liebman, "On New German Cinema, Art, Enlightenment, and the Public Sphere: An Interview with Alexander Kluge", *October*, 46 (Fall, 1988), p. 27. "So at night", Kluge states, "I see films that are different from my experiences during the day. Thus there is a strict separation between experience and the cinema. That is the obstacle for our films. For we are people of the '60s, and we do not believe in the opposition between experience and fiction".
**32** | Alexandra Kluge and Bion Steinborn, "Film ist das natürliche Tauschverhältnis der Arbeit...", *Filmfaust* 1.6 (December, 1977), p. 96.
**33** | Jan Dawson, "'But Why are the Questions so Abstract?,'" p. 34.
**34** | Stuart Liebman, "On New German Cinema, Art, Enlightenment, and the Public Sphere", p. 29.

If Kluge is also wary of conventional documentary film, it is because he has little faith in one of its defining tenets: that is, that the camera is able to provide the viewer with a truthful re-presentation of reality.[35] In keeping with Bertolt Brecht's criticism of photography in *The Threepenny Opera,* Kluge argues that documentary realism is incapable of capturing reality because the camera "can only photograph something that's present"[36]:

> On the subject of realism, Brecht says: Of what use is an exterior view of the AEG if I cannot see what is going on inside the building in terms of relationships, wage labour, capital, international investments – a photograph of the AEG says nothing about the AEG itself. Thus, as Brecht says, most of the real conditions have slipped into the functional. This is the heart of the problem of realism. If I conceive of realism as the knowledge of relationships [*eine Kenntnis von Zusammenhänge*], then I must provide a trope for what cannot be shown in the film, for what the camera cannot record.[37]

These "relationships" or *"Zusammenhänge"* (which can also aptly be described as "interconnections") refer not only, as per Brecht's example, to the alienated labour conditions and financial affiliations rendered invisible by the camera's so-called "objective" re-presentation of reality. Rather, they are associated more generally with the viewer's capacity to draw distinctions and form connections that are grounded in the experiences of the subject. As Kluge makes clear, "[m]ere documentation forecloses *Zusammenhang*" (that is, the context and/or capacity for interconnection). "[O]bjectivity", he adds,

---

**35** | "I don't", Kluge states, "believe too much in documentary realism: because it doesn't describe reality. The most ideological illusion of all would be to believe that documentary realism is realism". Dawson, "'But Why are the Questions so Abstract?'", p. 34.
**36** | Ibid., p. 35.
**37** | Alexander Kluge, "On Film and the Public Sphere", p. 46.

"does not exist without emotions, actions and desires, that is, without the eyes and the senses of the people involved."[38]

In Kluge's films, a number of techniques and devices are employed to generate *Zusammenhänge*, to stimulate the senses and, in the process, to both complicate and undermine the reality effect generated by the refined, organised and conventional form of much narrative and documentary cinema. In contrast to the harmonious structure that he associates with Hollywood film, the experimental form of Kluge's work generates contrast, ambiguity and tension that isn't easily resolved. The key device employed by Kluge in this regard is the "mixed" form according to which his films are constructed; an experimental aesthetic that consists of both documentary and fictional material that was either shot specifically for the film in question or gleaned from various sources including newsreels, books, paintings, photographs, drawings, and early cinema. By dissolving the traditional distinction between documentary and fictional film, by mixing black and white and colour footage, and by editing it together with intertitles, quotes, photographs, diagrams, and pictures, Kluge generates a series of contrasts and connections that disrupt the "unequivocal picture of reality" produced by both documentary and fictional film. For Kluge, this mixed aesthetic generates a more realistic representation of reality because the complex nature of the world it depicts challenges the idea that the reality in which we live is somehow immutable or set in stone. As Kluge makes clear, it is not he, the director, but reality itself which is responsible for generating this complexity.[39]

In order to remain true to the open, variable nature of real conditions, the montage practice favoured by Kluge is driven by a desire

---

**38** | Kluge quoted in Anton Kaes, "In Search of Germany: Alexander Kluge's The Patriot" in *Alexander Kluge: Raw Materials For the Imagination*, ed. Tara Forrest, p. 105.

**39** | Alexandra Kluge and Rainer Frey, "Interview mit Alexander Kluge. 'Eine realistische Haltung müßte der Zuschauer haben, müßte ich haben, müßte der Film haben", *Filmfaust* 20 (November, 1980), p. 20.

to stimulate the viewer's capacity to draw distinctions rather than channel or close meaning down. "We do not", he states, "fashion the associations of the viewers, that is what Hollywood does, we do not channel them at all, but we stimulate them, so that something independent comes into being, something which without these incentives, would not have been actualised".[40] This independent "third image" (which is manifested not in the film itself but rather in the head of the spectator who is watching it[41] is not an obvious association generated by two images that have been edited together to produce a connection conceived in advance by the director.[42] "We are not", Kluge states, "god over the materials. We do not provide a red thread to lead them through the film the way straightforward narratives do. [...] It requires another way of being involved. It's as if you are walking down the street and are looking at the windows." Viewers, he adds, "are required to think and make distinctions" for themselves.[43]

---

**40** | Rainer Lewandowski, "Interview" in: *Die Filme von Alexander Kluge*, ed. Rainer Lewandowski, Hildesheim and New York: Olms Presse, 1980, p. 36. See also Florian Rötzer, "Kino und Grabkammer: Gespräch mit Alexander Kluge" in: *Die Schrift an der Wand: Alexander Kluge: Rohstoffe und Materialien*, ed. Christian Schulte, Osnabrück: Universitätsverlag Rasch, 2000, p. 35.

**41** | This idea of the film in the spectator's head is regularly discussed by Kluge. See, for example, Edgar Reitz, Alexander Kluge and Wilfried Reinke, "Word and Film", *October*, 46 (Fall, 1988), p. 87 and Alexander Kluge, "Interview von Ulrich Gregor", p. 227.

**42** | Elaborating on this point, Kluge claims that "[t]his is basically no different from the situation where poets write poems and schoolchildren are forced to memorise them – why on earth should people with a phantasy of their own be forced to learn something by heart which was conceived in an associative fashion by somebody else?". Kluge, "On Film and the Public Sphere", p. 48.

**43** | Stuart Liebman, "On New German Cinema, Art, Enlightenment, and the Public Sphere," p. 55.

Film, in this context, is thus transformed from a medium that captures or fixes reality to a propaedeutic that hones and stimulates the audience's own capacity to interrogate reality by encouraging them to form connections and draw distinctions that are grounded in their own imagination, reality, and experience. As Kluge makes clear: "either social history narrates its novel of reality without regard for men or men narrate their counter-history. They can only do this, however, on the level of the complexity of reality. This demands in the most literal sense the 'art object', an aggregate of art objects. Sensuousness as method is not a natural product of society."[44]

## "A REALIST DRILLS"[45]

It is a book about cooperation, a wish. David and Goliath. How associative do human powers have to be [...] in order to shoot the monster of reality in the eye.[46]

The above quote appears in Kluge's foreword to *Die Patriotin* (*The Patriot*): a book which, like his film of the same title, was released in 1979 and which contains a text list, a series of stills, quotes, and other raw materials (such as photographs, drawings, stories, and newspaper clippings) that relate to and stimulate thinking about the issues and ideas explored in the film. Although the quote summarises what, for Kluge, is the driving force of the collection, it is also an apt description of the experimental impulse motivating both the film and its protagonist Gabi Teichert: a high school history teacher and a realist in the positive sense described by Kluge because she is

---

**44** | Alexander Kluge, "The Sharpest Ideology: That Reality Appeals to its Realistic Character", p. 196.
**45** | Alexander Kluge, "The Political as Intensity of Everyday Feelings" in *Alexander Kluge: Raw Materials for the Imagination*, p. 287.
**46** | Alexander Kluge, *Die Patriotin: Texte/Bilder 1-6*, Frankfurt am Main: Zweitausendeins, 1979, p. 7.

passionate about encouraging her students reflect on how -and with what effects – the reality in which they live could be transformed into something different.

For both Teichert and Kluge the so-called "probable" order of events around which linear accounts of history are constructed has a direct impact on shaping our conception of the possibilities and limitations of the present. As Kluge makes clear, what is problematic about these narratives is not only their carefully crafted, linear structure, but the extent to which both the process of exclusion out of which they are fashioned and the ideology of historical necessity through which they are rendered meaningful prohibit our capacity to conceive of the possibilities of the past, the present and the future in different terms. Why, Kluge asks, do

> we carry in us such a fixed conception of the probable order of events, which is only the sum of what is impressed upon us by the objective history or the media? Why do we hang onto it so energetically, while the imagination circles elsewhere [... and while] the sum of improbabilities is just as great as the sum of all probabilities?[47]

For Kluge, central to this idea of historical probability is a conception of historical realism that could more accurately be described as "historical fiction".[48] In a similar vein to his analysis of the limitations generated by the reality principle governing the political sphere, he argues that "[w]hat you notice as realistic [...] is not necessarily or certainly real. The potential and the historical roots, and the detours of possibilities, also belong to reality. The realistic result, the actual result, is only an abstraction that has murdered all other possibilities for the moment."[49]

---

47 | Claus Philipp, "Vertrauenswürdige Irrtümer: Ein Gespräch", p. 10.
48 | Alexander Kluge, "The Sharpest Ideology: That Reality Appeals to its Realistic Character", p. 191.
49 | Jan Dawson, "'But Why are the Questions so Abstract?'", p. 34.

Teichert too is deeply dissatisfied with the highly abstract, linear narratives that appear in the textbooks assigned to her students, so much so that she heads out of the classroom and into the field in search of forgotten, overlooked, and discarded materials with which she can rejuvenate the history curriculum and, in the process, encourage her students to reflect on the "porosity" of both the past and the present.[50] Armed with various tools (including a shovel, a telescope, a saw, and a drill) she works like an archaeologist unearthing materials; she studies the moon; and she sets up a laboratory replete with test tubes and beakers in which she boils text, saws into books, and drills holes into the tightly organized linear narratives around which the history curriculum is constructed.

*Figure 1: The Patriot*

---

**50** | "I don't", Kluge notes, "believe in the existing circumstances; rather, I believe in the porosity of the existing situation, at least when I can make it out". Stuart Liebman, "On New German Cinema, Art, Enlightenment, and the Public Sphere", p. 38.

As Miriam Hansen has pointed out, "Gabi Teichert's work [...] is the work of the film itself"[51] and *The Patriot* is constructed, in part, out of the kind of raw materials that Teichert may have unearthed as a result of her experimental approach. In keeping with Kluge's realistic method, these materials (which include photographs, poems, maps, interviews, sketches, diagrams, illustrations from fairytales, voiceover statements, intertitles and newsreel footage) are edited together in a manner which stimulates the senses and facilitates an active, creative mode of engagement via which the solidity of reality is called into question.

Both Teichert and Kluge are driven by a desire to "see things in their *Zusammenhang*"[52]; that is, their context and/or interconnection and, in the process, to rupture the neat facade of consistency generated by historical documents (or "novel[s] of reality") that seek to bolster and/or naturalise politically motivated agendas, policies, and decisions. As Walter Benjamin makes clear: "The rulers at any time are the heirs of all those who have been victorious throughout history". Historical documents that emphasise the probability and rigidity of both the past and the present can, in this sense, be seen as a form of "empathy with the victor" because their delineation of politically motivated decisions and events as stepping stones in history's so-called march of progress to the future creates a climate within which it is difficult to conceive of the possibilities of the past, the present, and the future beyond the "realistic" paradigm established and maintained by the ruling status quo.[53]

As Kluge's voiceover states in the opening sequence of the film, Teichert is a "patriot" because "she takes an interest in all the dead of

---

**51** | Miriam Hansen, "Alexander Kluge, Cinema and the Public Sphere: The Construction Site of Counter-History", *Discourse*, 6 (1983), p. 70.
**52** | Kluge, *Die Patriotin*, p. 18.
**53** | Walter Benjamin, "Paralipomena to 'On the Concept of History'" in: Walter Benjamin, *Selected Writings: Volume 4, 1938-1940*, ed. Howard Eiland and Michael W. Jennings, Cambridge, Mass. and London, England: Harvard University Press, 2003, p. 406.

the Reich" – an interest which (as revealed by her activities throughout the course of the film) is focused on redeeming those materials, memories, feelings, and wishes that give voice to "generations of men who the whole time actually wanted and want something completely different".[54] When criticized by her colleague for her lack of order and so-called inability to construct a "rational argument", she responds simply by stating that she isn't "cold hearted". In other words: she is neither able to professionally divorce, nor analytically distance herself from the unfulfilled possibilities, hopes, and wishes (what Kluge describes as "subjunctive realities") that have been excised from the neat, linear histories she is expected to teach in the classroom. As the voiceover states over footage of Teichert marking essays at her desk one Sunday morning, when she is reading her students' assignments, she is duty-bound to cross out the "errors", even though the mistakes that give voice to alternative possibilities are, for Teichert, "the best parts".

*Figure 2: The Patriot*

**54** | Kluge, "The Political as Intensity of Everyday Feeling", p. 190.

Teichert's energies are, however, not limited to excavating the past in search of untapped possibilities. Rather, she is also committed to participating in and actively contributing to contemporary activities, debates, and events that could have a future impact on transforming both history and the curriculum for the better. For example, in a section of *The Patriot* entitled "Die Parteitag" (Party Conference), we view Teichert at a Convention of the Social Democrats where the delegates are involved, in part, in debating the formation of policy on issues pertaining to nuclear power. "If", Kluge's voiceover states, "Gabi Teichert is to teach German history, then she wants to actually participate in decisions made, such as those here at this event. She must try to influence the delegates".

In the following scenes, we view Teichert in discussions with a number of real politicians who are clearly unaware that she is a fictional character and that their discussions are being shot for Kluge's film. After introducing herself to the delegates as a teacher who wants to change history and thus the curriculum for the better, she claims that "the material available for advanced history lessons isn't positive enough because our German history isn't positive enough either". As revealed, however, throughout the course of the film, Teichert's conception of a more "positive" curriculum is based not on the replacement of a negative chain of events with a narrative that is more pleasant in its focus, but on the opening up of the subject to incorporate materials that could challenge her students to question the extent to which the history of their country (and, by extension, the present reality in which they live) could have turned out very differently. "It would be bad", Teichert states, "if that which is known about the history of my country were ultimately the truth. There is always a way out".

It is this desire to find a "way out" that is the driving impetus of the realistic method underpinning the construction of Kluge's films; a method which employs both montage and a mixed aesthetic to reinvigorate the senses, to sharpen perception, and to encourage viewers to become active, imaginative participants in the meaning-making process. For example, in the opening minutes of *The Patriot*, we are presented with a montage of materials that includes a black and white image of Teichert's face; intertitles; fictional footage of a battlefield littered with corpses; a poem by Christian Morgenstern recited by Kluge in voiceover; an image of the earth and the sun rotating in unison; and a drawing – reminiscent of a fairytale image – of a man trying in vain to scale the icy landscape that would lead him to a castle. These images are followed by sketches of soldiers walking though a snowy landscape, tanks in battle, bodies blasted helplessly into the air, and men digging trenches in Stalingrad. All the while we hear the voice of "the knee" – a character inspired by the Morgenstern poem in which the uninjured knee of a dead soldier travels alone through the world. "No one", the knee states in voiceover, "is actually dead when he dies. You can't just write us off: the wishes, the legs, the many joints, ribs, skin that freezes. And if only I remain, the knee, then I must speak, speak, speak."

The figure of the knee is an interesting inclusion, not least because it is an embodied example of the hopes and wishes of human beings that are sidelined by approaches to the representation and writing of history that are more conventional in their content and structure. When Kluge speaks via the voice of the knee of the "wishes", the "ribs", and the "skin that freezes", he is invoking "the anti-realism of feelings"[55]; that is, the desire for happiness and the capacity for protest that, for Kluge, is embodied at a cellular level in generations of human experience and which is manifested in the instinctual capacity to draw distinctions based on our sense of how things *should* be.[56]

"The knee", as Anton Kaes has pointed out (which is "anatomically nothing more than a joint that makes movement possible") can also be read "as a concrete image for the 'between'" and as "an alle-

---

**55** | Laudenbach,'"Träume sind die Nahrung auf dem Weg zum Ziel"', p. 2.

**56** | "Our cells", Kluge notes, "are around four million years old, our eyes have experience that comprises the complete history of the world". Jürgen Bevers, Klaus Kreimeier und Jutta Müller, "'Eine Baustelle ist vorteilhafter als ganze Häuser': Ein Gespräch mit Alexander Kluge," *Spuren: Zeitschrift für Kunst und Gesellschaft* I (Februar/März, 1980), p. 18.

gory for montage and *Zusammenhang*". Quoting Kluge, Kaes adds: "I developed the knee [...] from this Morgenstern poem. You never see it except in the gap between the shots [...] and that is the point: the main things in the film are between the shots".[57] While Kluge's montage practice functions to open up gaps within which the viewer can "fly into the break"[58], as demonstrated by Teichert's visit to the SPD conference, contrast, space and tension are also generated by the manner in which Kluge shoots footage of fictional characters interacting with real people, events, and situations. In *The Patriot* what is made immediately apparent from the uncomfortable reactions of the participants with whom Teichert converses is the "inappropriateness" of voicing one's wishes and desires in a political context that functions according to its own rules, regulations, and logic. As Teichert sits despondently on the steps outside the auditorium where the SPD delegates are discussing issues pertaining to energy policy that will have a serious impact on the future of Germany, Kluge's voiceover states: "For one thousand years, governments have been structured so I can only vote for what I want, by accepting what I don't want."

It is the gap illustrated in this sequence – between the hopes, feelings, and desires of individuals and a status quo both produced and sustained by politicians, institutions, and the media – that highlights "the contrast between the wishes of people and a reality which does not answer these wishes".[59] By inserting fictional characters into so-called real contexts, Kluge seeks to generate a scenario within which the "realism of the senses" (in the form of "the eyes, the ears, the head of a real person"[60]) can exert a "practical critique"[61] of

---

57 | Kaes, "In Search of Germany", pp. 120-121.
58 | Kluge, "Interview von Ulrich Gregor", p. 236.
59 | Kluge, "The Political as Intensity of Everyday Feeling", p. 284.
60 | Alexander Kluge, "Reibungsverluste: Gespräch mit Klaus Eder (1980)" in: Kluge, *In Gefahr und größter Not*, ed. Christian Schulte, p. 245.
61 | Alexander Kluge and Klaus Eder, "Debate on the Documentary Film: Conversation with Klaus Eder, 1980" in: *Alexander Kluge: Raw Materials for the Imagination*, p. 198.

the reality principle governing the political sphere. What is powerful and, at times, also comical about Teichert's presence at the SPD conference is the degree to which her comments, hopes, suggestions, and ideas ruffle the veil of realism in which the legitimacy of the status quo is cloaked.

## FEELINGS, POLITICS, *WAR AND PEACE*

The bombers remind us of what Leonardo da Vinci expected of man in flight: that he was to ascend to the skies 'in order to seek snow on the mountaintops and bring it back to the city to spread on the sweltering streets in summer.[62]

If, Kluge argues, "politics had all the feelings at its disposal" then it "would be strong enough to prevent wars, to nip Fascism in the bud rather than defeating it after it had done its worst".[63] The problem lies, however, in the gap that separates the senses from the political and historical spheres: "The big decisions in history", he writes, "are not made in the realm of what we can experience close at hand. The big disasters take place in the distance which we cannot experience, for which we don't have the appropriate telescopes (or microscopes) in our senses". The two worlds "don't come together. In this sense man is not a social, not a political being".[64]

Kluge's analysis of this experience of sensory alienation builds on and develops ideas explored by Walter Benjamin in his epilogue to 'The Work of Art in the Age of Mechanical Reproduction' in which he draws a distinction between the aestheticisation of politics undertaken by fascism and the significant role that art can play in

---

[62] | Pierre-Maxime Schuhl quoted in Walter Benjamin, *The Arcades Project*, Cambridge, Mass., and London, England: Harvard University Press, 1999, p. 486.
[63] | Hopf, '"Feelings Can Move Mountains..."', p. 243.
[64] | Kluge, "The Political as Intensity of Everyday Feeling", p. 285.

both revitalising the senses and rejuvenating the viewer's capacity for imagination, experience, and autonomous thought. The aestheticisation of war enacted by fascism has, Benjamin writes, "reached the point where [humankind] can experience its own annihilation as a supreme aesthetic pleasure"[65] – a point illustrated via a quote from the 'Futurist Manifesto' in which war is described as "beautiful because it combines gunfire, barrages, cease-fires, scents, and the fragrance of putrefaction into a symphony."[66]

The aestheticisation of politics that Benjamin is referring to here is not, of course, specific to Fascism but is a practice which is alive and well in the contemporary media and which functions – as per the armoury that Kluge associates with the reality principle – to anaesthetise and thereby seal the subject off from the events and ideas it is depicting. As Kluge and Oskar Negt argue in *Public Sphere and Experience,* the "abstract character" and entertainment-driven focus of news and current affairs programs prohibits the viewer from relating – in an engaged, sensual, and intuitive manner – with the issues and ideas in question.[67]

*War and Peace* is one of three collaborative films co-directed by Kluge that was produced in direct response to political events that were taking place in West Germany at the time. Co-produced by Kluge, Volker Schlöndorff, Stefan Aust, and Heinrich Böll[68], the film explores the relationship between war and peace, freedom and

---

65 | Walter Benjamin, "The Work of Art in the Age of its Technological Reproducibility" in: Benjamin, *Selected Writings: Volume 4*, p. 270. On this topic, see Susan Buck-Morss' essay "Aesthetics and Anaesthetics: Walter Benjamin's Artwork Essay Reconsidered", *New Formations*, 20 (Summer, 1993), pp. 123-143.

66 | Emilio Filippo Tommaso Marinetti quoted in Benjamin, "The Work of Art in the Age of its Technological Reproducibility", p. 269.

67 | Oskar Negt and Alexander Kluge, *Public Sphere and Experience: Toward an Analysis of the Bourgeois and Proletarian Public Sphere*, Minneapolis and London: University of Minnesota Press, 1993, p. 119.

68 | The film also contains a contribution by Axel Engstfeld.

subjugation, and the dangers faced by the FRG (and Europe more generally) as a direct result of the American installation of nuclear weapons on West German soil. As Aust has made clear, his participation in the venture was driven by a desire "to do what you cannot do (or cannot do any longer) in television, to try new forms, to sharpen the content, to become involved in the pressing political problems of the day, take a position and demonstrate connections [*Zusammenhänge darstellen*]".[69] "[W]e believe", Schlöndorff states,

> that our gaze is different from the gaze of the television camera, and different than, earlier, the gaze of the *Wochenschau*; if later someone wants to produce a chronicle of our time, then we prefabricate, so to speak, material that has a different kind of sensuousness [*Sinnlichkeit*], a different gaze and a perhaps also a different personality.[70]

As the directors make clear, the experimental form of the film is driven by a desire to rob the status quo of what Kluge describes as its "reality character"[71] and, in doing so, to reinvest the audience with the capacity to determine what is and isn't possible, desirable, and/or real. Instead of presenting the audience with a one-sided, pre-processed analysis in which the case for or against the stockpiling of nuclear weapons is laid out in a clear and didactic fashion, the mixed form

---

**69** | Stefan Aust quoted in Hans-Bernard Moeller and George Lellis, *Volker Schlöndorff's Cinema: Adaption, Politics, and the 'Movie-Appropriate'*, Carbondale and Edwardsville: Southern Illinois University Press, 2002, p. 192. See also Stefan Aust's discussion of the film in Alexander Kluge, "Am Kältesten Punkt des Kalten Kriegs/Stephan Aust über ein Beispiel des Rüstungs-Wahns", *Primetime/Spätausgabe*, RTL, 29 October, 2006.
**70** | Klaus Eder and Peter Hamm, "Reise in der Wirklichkeit: Ein Gespräch mit Alexander Kluge und Volker Schlöndorff über das Projekt eines Krieg- und Frieden-Films", *Kirche und Film*, 3 (März, 1982), p. 6.
**71** | Bion Steinborn, "'Unser Herrgott ist der erste Kernaggressor': Ein Gespräch mit Alexander Kluge und Volker Schlöndorff über (den Film) 'Krieg und Frieden'", *Filmfaust*, 32 (Februar-März, 1983), p. 20.

of the film (which consists of new, old, fictional and documentary footage, images, quotes, and diagrams, clips from video games, political speeches and instructional videos, interviews with missile testers, military strategists and "the father of the neutron bomb") seeks to facilitate *Zusammenhänge* and, in the process, to undo the experience of sensorial alienation that Kluge associates with the reality principle.

Figure 3: War and Peace

The aestheticisation of politics described by Benjamin, and the anaesthetisation of the senses with which he associates it, is explored by the film on a number of different levels, most notably through the contrast it establishes (as early as the pre-title opening sequence) between the different modes of perception and experience facilitated by distant and proximate relationships. In one scene, for example, we are presented with stuttering black and white footage of two enemy soldiers who unexpectedly find themselves sharing a trench. "Initially", Kluge's voiceover informs us, "one enemy wanted to stab the other enemy to death". After realising, however, that one of them is seriously wounded, the other places a cigarette in his enemy's mouth, but he dies before he has the opportunity to smoke it. "They only knew each other for ten minutes", the voiceover states, and the scene cuts first to an image of Gabi Teichert's eye and then to colour-tinted footage of a battleship in motion with sailors scrambling across the deck. "Fourteen seconds", Kluge states over an image of a star-spangled sky, "was how long the battleship had before the rocket hit. One doesn't get to know each other at all."

This distinction – between modes of violence that are, on the one hand, mediated by and, on the other hand, completely devoid of human contact – is explored in detail throughout the film in a manner that speaks directly to Kluge's delineation of the degree to which our relationship to the political sphere, and warfare in particular, is mediated by an experience of sensorial galvanisation that prohibits us from feeling the pain of others and acting according to our own best interests. While the scenario in the trench certainly isn't devoid of irony (the soldier initially decides to kill his enemy but refrains from doing so once he realises he is hurt) the shift from face to face combat to long distance warfare illustrated by this sequence forms part of a historical trajectory traced by the film, albeit in a discontinuous way: a trajectory which is buttressed by technological "progress" and which enables us, in the words of Benjamin, to "experience our own destruction as an aesthetic pleasure."

This shift – from close to long distance warfare, from personal contact to no contact at all – is also explored later in the film via a segment that opens with the following quote: "In former times people were closer. Firearms didn't reach that far". This on-screen statement is succeeded by black and white footage of bomber planes during the Second World War. We watch the planes swoop and dive as they drop bombs high above their patchwork targets, and then the film cuts to reveal the shocking reality of the attacks for those located on the ground. We see exploding bombs, burning buildings, and people frantically trying to escape the area by foot, via tank, and on horseback. The air is thick with panic, fire and smoke, cars roll off the road, and horses buckle under pressure only to be trampled on by other horses, soldiers, vehicles, and carts. This scene of destruction is intercut with images of a bomber pilot's perspective shot from a camera located in the cockpit. As the plane dives, the abstract target looms before our gaze before it is clouded in a haze of smoke generated by the bomb as it is released from the plane. From the pilot's bird's eye perspective, there is little sense of connection between his/her aerial manoeuvres and the invisible horror taking place on the ground, the only trace of which is manifested in a smoky haze which is barely perceptible from on high.[72]

As *War and Peace* makes clear, the gap explored in this sequence – between the anaesthetised gaze of the pilot and the sensations of fear, terror, and panic experienced first hand from below – is exacerbated by nuclear warfare and the development of atomic weapons designed to generate destruction from afar. As the voiceover makes clear in the early stages of the film, a number of these weapons have been stockpiled on both sides of the East/West German border by Soviet and US military forces. "We are a sovereign state", the voiceover claims over footage of trucks transporting nuclear weapons. "Our security is ensured by the Americans. For this they've brought some equipment into our country".

This "equipment" is displayed throughout the course of the film via different types of footage: We view ads produced by arms manufacturers, images of nuclear tests conducted in the Nevada desert, and a remote military site in West Germany surrounded by barbed wire

---

[72] | This lack of connection is also demonstrated in *The Patriot* via a series of clips of American bomber pilots shot during the Second World War. For example, in one sequence, we view footage of bomber planes flying high above their targets which is intercut with images shot from a pilot's perspective of bombs reminiscent of fireflys being released onto the houses below. This is followed by footage of bomber pilots back at their base standing in front of their plane and talking and laughing among themselves, while Kluge states in voiceover: "These bomber pilots are back from their mission. They haven't experienced Germany. They've simply been razing the country for eighteen hours".

## Subjunctive Realism: Kluge on Film, Politics, and Feelings

and electric fences which is used for the storage of nuclear warheads. Outside the storage facility a group of protesters gathers in the cold bearing signs that state: "No nuclear missiles in the BRD" and "Peace only exists without weapons." What is clear, however, is that this conception of peace stands in stark contrast to the image of a peaceful existence propagated by the US president, Ronald Reagan, whom we view via public appearances and press conferences with German Chancellor Helmut Kohl. Over footage of a German family wearing protective suits in a barren, windswept landscape, the voiceover states: "Our freedom, so we learned, was based on nuclear deterrence".

This and other dystopian images of a post-nuclear European landscape are contrasted with footage of what might have been because "once upon a time", the voiceover states, "we had different ideas". In a sequence that evokes the utopian promise of the epigraph that opens this section (in which flying machines would gather snow from the mountains to be sprinkled over hot city streets) we see how German weapons were repurposed in the postwar period for humanitarian (rather than military) ends. We learn, for example, that submarine hulls were transformed into silos for the storage of grain while artillery shells metamorphosised into ovens, cups and pots for domestic use. The sense of promise contained in these objects is, however, counteracted by footage depicting the remilitarisation of West Germany in the form of nuclear canons and submarines brought into the country by the US government in order to defend their interests on West German soil. "No one asked us", the voiceover claims. "Our security and our lives are dictated by military experts and other people of questionable competence".

One such figure is Sam Cohen who appears in an interview conducted in the private spaces of his car and his Californian home and whose "competence" is bound with his status as the inventor of the neutron bomb. In between drinking coffee and preparing cocktails in the kitchen while his wife cooks dinner on the stove, Cohen explains – in a proud, matter-of-fact tone – how the neutron bomb is highly effective at killing people without, ironically, destroying the infrastructure upon which they rely. The bomb, he explains, is designed to explode 2000 or 3000 feet above the ground. "The explosion releases all these neutrons, this radiation. Just like a giant X-ray machine" so that the people below are completely irradiated. "It's by far", he states proudly while drawing on a cigarette, "the most effective weapon ever invented. That sounds boastful but it's true. There has never been anything like it."

What is disturbing about this sequence is the extreme, almost pathological indifference displayed by Cohen in regard to the effects that his invention would, once detonated, have on real people located on the ground; an indifference also exhibited by his wife (who focuses her energies on "tennis" and "the house") and his children who actually echo the phrase "tremendous indifference" to characterise their relationship to their father's work. When the German interviewer notes that he is not indifferent because the nuclear battlefield Cohen is describing is situated in Europe, ie. his home, Cohen responds cooly by stating: "Of course. Unfortunately the Europeans live adjacent to the Soviet Bloc. The threat is against Europe, not America." This sense of detachment and indifference is also communicated in a scene located in a munitions firm responsible for the production and testing of the Pershing II: "the first missile to be able to reach Moscow from German soil". When asked about his work, a company employee notes that missile testing is "just a business. It is just like testing cars. [...] I personally don't feel any connection to war or anything like that."

It is precisely this lack of connection – between arms producers and the targets of such weaponry, between bomber pilots and the horror of death, between nuclear "deterrence" and the human effects wreaked by a nuclear strike – that the film seeks to break down by cutting through the sense of abstraction via which such distance and indifference are maintained. The kind of cool detachment exhibited, for example, in the missile tester's comments is complicated by a radio report in which a doctor reflects on the type of injuries that would be sustained as a result of a nuclear attack. "Anyone", he states,

who looks at a fireball from thirty miles away, his retina will burn and he will go blind. There would be tens of thousands of third degree burns [...].

There would be skull fractures, ruptured lungs, spinal injuries, lacerations and hemorrhages. Even at eleven or twelve miles, ordinary windows would become deadly weapons. Glass shards flying at ninety miles an hour will kill everyone in the room.

Later in the film, an image of a mushroom cloud rising in the sky is followed by a German instructional video detailing how to react in the case of a nuclear explosion. "When caught outdoors", the adviser states, "carry out the following procedures: Shield eyes from the bright light and drop to the ground." In another segment, we view footage of people gathering together in protective masks followed by the on-screen instruction: "Stay at home". An animated diagram of weaponry appears and is followed by a map indicating how long it would take for nuclear missiles to reach several West German cities after crossing the East German border: Four minutes to Munich, seven to Stuttgart, and one to Hamburg. ie. not a lot of time for people below to prepare.

*Figure 4: War and Peace*

## STRATEGIES FROM ABOVE AND BELOW

Kluge's preoccupation with the imbalance of power exhibited in this and other sequences – between the "strategies from above" enacted by those in positions of power and the scant opportunities available for "strategies from below"[73]- stems, in part, from his own experience of surviving the bombing of his hometown Halberstadt at the end of the Second World War; an event documented in his literary montage piece 'The Air Raid on Halberstadt, 8 April 1945'.[74] One of the characters who features in this fragmentary text is Gerda Baethe whose story is discussed in class by Teichert's history students in *The Patriot* and who finds herself in an air raid shelter with little means available to protect her children. "The problem", Kluge notes in a different context in which he extrapolates on this story,

> is that the woman in the bomb-cellar in 1944, for example, has no means at all to defend herself in that moment. She might perhaps have had means in 1928 if she had organised with others *before* the development which then moves towards Papen, Schleicher and Hitler. So the question of organization is located in 1928, and the requisite consciousness is located in 1944.[75]

---

73 | For Kluge's analysis of the differences between these two strategies, see "The Political as Intensity of Everyday Feeling", p. 289.
74 | Alexander Kluge, "Der Luftangriff auf Halberstadt am 8. April 1945" in: Alexander Kluge, *Neue Geschichten. Hefte 1-18: 'Unheimlichkeit der Zeit'*, Frankfurt am Main: Suhrkamp, 1978, pp. 33-106. For Kluge's comments in this regard, see Bion Steinborn, "'Unser Herrgott ist der erste Kernaggressor': Ein Gespräch mit Alexander Kluge und Volker Schlöndorff über (den Film) 'Krieg und Frieden'", *Filmfaust*, 32 (Februar-März, 1983), p. 20. For a comprehensive analysis of these "strategies" in relation to the Halberstadt piece, see David Roberts, "Alexander Kluge and German History: 'The Air Raid on Halberstadt on 8.4.1945'", in *Alexander Kluge: Raw Materials For the Imagination*, pp. 127-154.
75 | Kluge, "The Political as Intensity of Everyday Feeling," pp. 289-290.

As noted previously, Kluge reads this experience of delayed consciousness as a symptom of the pervasive conception of "politics as a specialised area that others look after for us and not as a degree of intensity of our own feelings".[76] By deferring important decision-making responsibilities to politicians and the mainstream media, the public – in this context – occupies a position of both distance and indifference from the very real effects generated by "strategies from above". While Gerda Baethe's story is a very concrete example of the kind of helplessness that Kluge and his family must have felt living in Halberstadt during the war, it also functions as an allegory for the imbalance of power and the experience of alienation that, for Kluge, characterises the disjunction between politics and the public in the twentieth and twenty-first centuries. As he makes clear:

if this relationship of person/bomb in the emergency is the model of how our modern world intends to deal with people and if we don't want to deceive ourselves in times of peace or apparent peace about the fact that this is precisely the point of the emergency, then we must ask ourselves whether there are any reasons which make us satisfied with the meagre means of a strategy from below in the emergency.[77]

Kluge's approach (as prefigured in the comparison with David and Goliath cited above) is to undo, complicate, and undermine the veracity of the behemoth of reality generated by those who develop "strategies from above" to support and maintain their own interests. "Politicians", Heinrich Böll states in footage in *War and Peace* shot at a political rally in Bonn, have the capacity to "turn us into complacent cynics. It's easily done. They can have a paralysed population around the globe, paralysed by weapons, this plague of weapons".

In scenes that follow we view the public staging of political reality in the form of footage capturing the media's documentation of

---

76 | Ibid., p. 289.
77 | Ibid.

the arrival by helicopter of senior political figures at an international economic summit in France. At the moment each helicopter lands, a band pipes up with military music, fountains that were previously dormant majestically ascend in the background, and two men roll out a red carpet that will lead the dignitaries – who are engaged in heavily staged "casual" conversation – from the helicopter to the cavalcade awaiting them. Later we are presented with footage of politicians seated at a table in "Le Salon de la Paix" at the Palace of Versailles surrounded by the international media while a news bulletin announces: "3.09pm: More than 20,000 Israeli soldiers backed up by tanks are attacking Lebanon".

As the following voiceover statement makes clear, the staging of political reality enacted by politicians and the media plays a significant role in both generating and augmenting the sense of paralysis described by Kluge and Böll. "Our curiosity", the voiceover states,

must constantly be fed by fresh news from the media. New suffering as well. In this sense, we are cannibals. But our feelings can not easily adjust to the suffering of others. Feeling takes time. The war machine, however, apparently functions timelessly. On the one hand, it doggedly carries out the same war. On the other hand, it changes scenes so abruptly, that the feelings can't follow. One moment it's Pershing, then it's Poland, then the Falklands, now it's Lebanon.

In the following sequence, we view a montage of clips of the destruction wrought on the ground in Lebanon as a direct result of strategies conceived from above. We see demolished buildings, hills of rubble, a burnt-out hotel devoid of windows, a female beggar, abandoned cars, and a young man who stares pensively at the camera. The scene then cuts back to the Palace of Versailles where political leaders are dining in the sumptuous surroundings of the Hall of Mirrors encircled by the international media who are there to capture the "refined", "civilised" manner in which politicians participate in such activities.

What is significant about *War and Peace* is the manner in which it ruptures the veneer of refinement generated by these and other images, not by producing a coherent counter-narrative, but by collating an experimental assemblage of materials that prompts the audience to generate questions and draw connections but which resists the impulse towards didacticism, lucidity and closure characteristic of Hollywood cinema and the mainstream news media. In the final minutes of the film, we are presented with a fast-paced panorama of a landscape shot from a train, the green fields of which are punctuated by nuclear power plants that flash up and disappear just as rapidly. "The nearly unsolvable problem", the directors state via the intertitle which follows, is "to avoid being struck dumb, whether through the power of others, or through one's own paralysis". If, as Kluge suggests, a realist film practice can shed light on this problem, then it is because he has faith in its capacity to motivate feelings, to rupture the sensorial and ideological armour generated by the reality principle and, in the process, to foster a form of embodied consciousness through which meaningful political engagement is enabled.

# CHAPTER 2

Creative Co-Productions:

Kluge's Television Experiments

---

Among the many stories contained in Alexander Kluge's book *Die Lücke, die der Teufel läßt* are several pieces in which Kluge describes a series of events that transpired when world leaders gathered together in Munich in 2003 to discuss international security policy.[1] In "Curiosity is my Profession: A Scientific Manager", Kluge describes the activities of a group of activists who have gathered in the cold outside the conference venue to protest against the US government's plans to establish a national missile defence program. One of the protestors, who is described as Berthold G., manages to slip past security and blend in among the waiters serving coffee to the conference delegates. His presence, however, does not escape the attention of Alois Becker: a "scientific manager" in the Taylorist tradition who

---

1 | Alexander Kluge, *Die Lücke, die der Teufel läßt: Im Umfeld des neuen Jahrhunderts*, Frankfurt am Main: Suhrkamp Verlag, 2003. A selection of the stories contained in this book has been published in English translation as Alexander Kluge, *The Devil's Blind Spot: Tales from the New Century*, New York: New Directions Books, 2004. The stories in question – which appear in a section entitled "Was heißt Macht?/Wem kann man trauen?" – do not appear in the English version. Some of them have, however, been translated into English. See Alexander Kluge, "At the 2003 International Security Conference" in: *Alexander Kluge: Raw Materials for the Imagination*, ed. Tara Forrest, Amsterdam: Amsterdam University Press, 2012, pp. 291-301.

works as a "productivity expert" for a car manufacturer. As Becker makes clear:

> The classical field of scientific management (or ergometry) was focused on production: how much time and effort is expended in what process to create what product. So, for instance, at this conference I am interested in the following distinction: how much brainpower goes into carrying out routine duties and moderation (sales discussions, lobbying, greeting, maintaining hierarchical relationships), and how much consists of critique.[2]

According to Becker, who has been observing the behaviour of the delegates, "92%" of their time and energy is expended in the performance of "routine duties and moderation", leaving a mere 8% for activities such as critique.[3] As Becker's comments make clear, the mode of labour exhibited by those who occupy the professional political sphere is divorced from the kind of activity that Kluge associates with meaningful forms of political engagement: "What goes on here is a concrete form of mental labour, one specializing in access, networking and consensus, where the traditional process of critique (the capacity to draw distinctions [Ünterscheidungsvermögen], self-certainty, control) does not play a role".[4] Bertold G. has, however, infiltrated the conference venue in an attempt to give voice to the protestors' criticism of the burgeoning "arms race in outer space". The US spy satellites, he states, "represent an even more dangerous provocation than the missile defense shield" and by sparking conversations with defence company lobbyists and military personnel, he hopes to cleave open a space in this consensus-driven forum within which the protesters' criticisms can be publicly aired.

---

2 | Kluge, "At the 2003 International Security Conference", note 1, p. 300.
3 | Ibid.
4 | Ibid., p. 295. Translation modified. See Alexander Kluge, *Die Lücke, die der Teufel läßt*: *Im Umfeld des neuen Jahrhunderts*, Frankfurt am Main: Suhrkamp Verlag, 2003, p. 520.

In a passage which illustrates the yawning gap between those who develop "strategies from above" and the sense of futility experienced by people "below", Bertold G. defends his undercover presence at the conference in the following terms: "[A]t least", he states, "I'm doing something. It's not *useless* to be here, just 50cm from all these decision makers. I've gotten as close as 20, or even 10cm away when the decision makers take sugar". Becker, however, has little faith in the idea that this forum could provide Berthold G. (who is dressed, after all, as a waiter rather than an "expert"[5]) with an opportunity to enact a form of critique that would have a meaningful impact on the proceedings at hand:

What, Becker asks, would Berthold G's small, freezing group have to do in order to exert some influence on this conference which, in the course of 24 hours, will chart a new course, even if no 'decision' emerges? It must be considered, Becker admits, that these 'friends of critique' are not interested in influence, but rather in the 'creation of an intellectual space in which thought processes are lateralized (placed on equal footing) and thus brought into contact with the subjective input of concrete individuals, so that they interact with human experience.[6]

The desire voiced in this passage – for the actualisation of a public sphere in which the thought processes surrounding political decisions and events are brought into contact with "human experience" – is the impetus driving the production of Kluge's experimental television programs. Underpinning his work in this field is the distinction he draws between the role and function of an active public sphere and the so-called "pseudo-public sphere"[7] generated by politicians and the mainstream media. In contrast to the value-laden im-

---

**5** | Ibid., p. 293.
**6** | Ibid., p. 295.
**7** | Alexander Kluge, "On Film and the Public Sphere" in: *Alexander Kluge: Raw Materials For the Imagination*, Amsterdam: Amsterdam University Press, 2012, p. 40.

age of reality generated by the "pseudo-public sphere" (which limits our capacity to conceive of the extent to which things could, in fact, be very different), Kluge argues that an active public sphere is an inclusive, dynamic, and collaborative space where people participate in the meaning-making process surrounding issues, policies, events and ideas which impact directly on their concerns and interests. "The public sphere", he writes, is "what one might call the factory of politics – its site of production and, as such, it forms "the basis for processes of social change".[8]

Kluge's reference to the public sphere as a "factory" in this context is not insignificant given the central role creative labour occupies in his delineation of the task of an active public sphere. In contrast, however, to the alienated mode of labour associated with the kind of factory work analysed by Becker (the automated, habitual qualities of which are reflected in the "routine" activities of the conference delegates), the form of production that Kluge is referring to here is based on an active, creative mode of engagement. It is, he argues, via "subjective input"[9] that people become active "producers of their own experience".[10] As Joseph Beuys has argued in a discussion which resonates strongly with Kluge's ideas in this context, the "task is to discover a new form of social order capable of making a different use of human faculties, of human work, and of productive power".[11]

---

**8** | Ibid., p. 41.
**9** | Alexander Kluge, "At the 2003 International Security Conference", p. 295.
**10** | Alexander Kluge, "Pact with a Dead Man (1984)" in: *West German Filmmakers on Film: Visions and Voices*, ed. Eric Rentschler, New York and London: Holmes & Meier, 1988, p. 236.
**11** | "Difesa della Natura: Discussion by Joseph Beuys" in: *Joseph Beuys: The Art of Cooking*, ed. Lucrezia De Domizio Durini, Milano: Edizioni Charta, 1999, p. 131.

The conception of work outlined by Beuys (in which productivity is aligned with creative capital[12]) is central to his delineation of the task of "social sculpture" and, more specifically, the role that art can play in facilitating thinking, feeling and debate about the possibility of social change.[13] "My objects", he writes, "are to be seen as stimulants for the transformation of the idea of sculpture, or of art in general. They should provoke thoughts about what sculpture can be and how the concept of sculpting can be extended to the invisible materials used by everyone".[14] Foremost among these "invisible materials" are the thoughts and associations that are generated when people actively participate in "moulding" the formation of policies, opinions and ideas. In contrast, for example, to mainstream news programs that seek to close down meaning by persuading the audience of the benefits of a particular "reality", policy or idea, Beuys' work is driven, in part, by the desire to stimulate public debate about the possibilities and limitations of the

**12** | Beuys describes his position in the following terms: "The concept of economic growth and the concept of capital and all that goes with it, does not really make the world productive". "There is", he adds, "only human capacity and what flows from it. And this can continually be discussed and explored in an ongoing dialogue between people, and lead to endless productivity that builds up and rebuilds the world". "Conversation with Joseph Beuys: What is Art?" in: *What is Art? Conversation with Joseph Beuys*, ed. Volker Harlan, Forest Row: Claireview, 2004, p. 27.

**13** | In a similar vein to Kluge, Beuys argues that thinking and feeling should not be conceived as capacities distinct from one another. "Creativity", he writes, "is the possibility to think, or what we might call thinking power. It is also a question of the creativity of feelings. When we talk about thinking powers, we immediately refer to our heads and brain, and when we talk about feeling powers, we refer to the heart and the parts of the body around it. In this way we have already begun to talk about two parts of a complex organism". Lucrezia De Domizio and Joseph Beuys, "Difesa della Natura", p. 130.

**14** | "Conversation with Joseph Beuys: What is art?", p. 9.

world in which we live. In an attempt to bypass the binary distinction according to which people are categorised as either "artists" or "non-artists"[15], Beuys famously declared that "everyone is an artist"[16] because "thinking is practically a sculptural process"; that is, "a truly creative achievement, engendered by the human being, by the individual himself, and not a process indoctrinated by some authority or other".[17]

Within this schema, if television is to play a role in "reshaping" the public sphere[18], then it must engage the audience not as spectators but as creative co-producers of the programs themselves by encouraging viewers to draw on their own capacity for creativity (what Beuys describes as "thinking power"[19]) in order to engage productively with the material on screen. In contrast to Theodor Adorno's delineation of popular cultural forms as '"non-productive correlate[s]" of mechanised forms of labour that do not involve the effort of concentration at all", Kluge argues that television can play a productive role in mobilising the active, creative participation of the viewer. The aim, he notes in regard to the experimental form of his programs, is to "strain" people's perceptual muscles.[20]

---

**15** | Ibid., p. 21.
**16** | Ibid., p. 9.
**17** | Ibid., p. 17.
**18** | Kluge, "The Sharpest Ideology: That Reality Appeals to its Realistic Character", p. 193.
**19** | Lucrezia De Domizio and Joseph Beuys, "Difesa della Natura" in: *Joseph Beuys: The Art of Cooking*, p. 130.
**20** | Astrid Deuber-Mankowsky and Giaco Schiesser, "In the Real Time of Feelings: Interview with Alexander Kluge" in: *Alexander Kluge: Raw Materials For the Imagination*, p. 352.

## An Alternative Television Practice

> It is old-fashioned to assume as they did in the 1930s that these struggles will be determined in the streets when there is a mass medium in every house that acts as a kind of window. Against such a power to convince millions through television, all conventional means are powerless. That means that I also have to produce for this window. I can only influence a mass medium through a counter-mass medium. An entire public sphere through a counter-public sphere.[21]
>
> ALEXANDER KLUGE

Kluge's move into the world of television was formalised in 1988 with the establishment of his Development Company for Television Programs (DCTP) – an organisation that was founded, in part, in response to the establishment, in 1984, of a "dual broadcasting system" in West Germany that saw the introduction of commercial television stations alongside the existing public service channels ARD and ZDF.[22] In an attempt to preserve, at least in part, the public

---

**21** | Stuart Liebman, "On New German Cinema, Art, Enlightenment, and the Public Sphere: An Interview with Alexander Kluge", *October* 46 (Fall, 1988), p. 40.

**22** | As Matthias Uecker has outlined in his study of Kluge's television programs, DCTP developed out of the *Arbeitsgemeinschaft für Kabel- und Satellitenprogramme*, an organization established by Kluge (together with a number of publishers, film directors, and theatre executives) in an attempt to create a "niche" for the so-called "old media" within the sphere of commercial television. The program *Die Stunde der Filmemacher (The Hour of the Filmmakers)*, which first screened on SAT 1 in 1985, developed of this alliance and showcased programs produced by German filmmakers that were overseen by Kluge, who served as the program's executive producer.

service ideals that had governed West German television up until that point, the then Social Democratic government (SPD) of North Rhine Westphalia instituted a new broadcasting law stipulating that all commercial stations seeking a broadcasting license for the state would need to provide programming slots for independent cultural producers. Benefitting from this law (and from Kluge's high profile in Germany as an award-winning author and filmmaker), DCTP was – together with SAT 1 and RTL (then RTL plus) – granted joint broadcasting licences that provided DCTP with weekly, commercial free programming slots; the strict independence of which was, and continues to be, safeguarded by the licensing contract.

Kluge's interest in the possibilities of an independent, experimental television practice was, however, signalled some years prior to the establishment of DCTP via his and Oskar Negt's book *Public Sphere and Experience* in which they discuss "the problem of television realism".[23] For Negt and Kluge, it is the emphasis on brevity and the cultivation of immediate comprehension characteristic, for example, of television news broadcasts which impacts negatively, not only on the viewer's capacity to assimilate news items by way of his/her experience, but on the viewer's ability to conceive of the meaning of a particular situation, issue, topic or event outside the terms within which it has been framed by the program. As Negt and Kluge make clear:

For a detailed account of the events that led to the establishment of these companies, see Chapter 1.3: "Prinzip Gegenproduktion: Alexander Kluge's 'Development Company for Television Programs (DCTP)'" in: Matthias Uecker, *Anti-Fernsehen? Alexander Kluge's Fernsehproduktionen*, Marburg: Schüren Verlag, 2000, pp. 48-63 and Gertrud Koch and Heide Schlüpmann, '"Nur Trümmern trau ich...": Ein Gespräch mit Alexander Kluge" in: *Kanalarbeit: Medienstrategien im Kulturwandel*, ed. Hans-Ulrich Reck, Basel and Frankfurt am Main: Stroemfeld and Roter Stern, 1998.

**23** | Oskar Negt and Alexander Kluge, *Public Sphere and Experience: Toward an Analysis of the Bourgeois and Proletarian Public Sphere*, Minneapolis and London: University of Minnesota Press, 1993, p. 128.

A sensational news item (for instance about an air disaster) is broadcast; but it is not accompanied by programs that might meaningfully interpret this news in light of social contradictions or develop it in relation to the viewer's own experience. It is only on such a broadened basis that grief, sympathy, incorporation into a historical context, or an autonomous reaction by the viewer become possible.[24]

The alternative conception of the possibilities of the medium outlined in *Public Sphere and Experience* takes as its starting point the need to replace the "pre-digested"[25] character of news and other so-called reality programs with formats that are genuinely organised around the active, creative participation of the audience. Drawing on Bertolt Brecht's analysis of the degree to which radio could be "transformed from an apparatus of distribution into one of communication"[26], Negt and Kluge argue that "the foundation of a possible emancipatory development of television must be organised around the creation of the "self-determination of the viewers".[27]

In keeping with Brecht's critique of photographic realism discussed in the previous chapter, Negt and Kluge argue that "[t]he mere reproduction of reality, for instance, the documentation of alienated labor"[28] is neither radical nor enabling in itself. "[P]eople",

---

**24** | Negt and Kluge, *Public Sphere and Experience*, p. 108.
**25** | "Pre-digested" is a term frequently employed by Adorno to describe the products of the Culture Industry: "The pre-digested quality of the product prevails, justifies itself and establishes itself all the more firmly in so far as it constantly refers to those who cannot digest anything not already pre-digested. It is baby food". Theodor W. Adorno, "The Schema of Mass Culture" in: *The Culture Industry: Selected Essays on Mass Culture*, ed. J.M. Bernstein, London and New York: Routledge, 2001, p. 67.
**26** | Brecht quoted in Negt and Kluge, *Public Sphere and Experience*, note 9, p. 103 and Brecht, "The Radio as Communicative Apparatus" in: *Bertolt Brecht on Film and Radio*, ed. Mark Silberman, London: Methuen, 2001, pp. 41-46.
**27** | Negt and Kluge, *Public Sphere and Experience*, p. 103.
**28** | Ibid., p. 128.

they argue, "can derive pleasure from the appropriation of this experience only if they can actively transform the circumstances that oppress them. It is from such a possibility of action alone that interest in realism can be aroused".[29] If, as Negt and Kluge argue, our heavily mediated relationship to the world of politics is an alienated one – insofar as we are passive consumers of, rather than active participants in the political sphere – then the task of an experimental television practice is to encourage the audience to become active participants in the political process. "The reshaping of the public sphere", Kluge writes, "is therefore the condition and at the same time that most important object which the realistic method works on and against". As he makes clear, "the uncompromising production of realistic products is itself the means of changing the horizon of experience by breaking through the limits of the public sphere".[30]

## THE PROGRAMS

Kluge's television programs – which include *News & Stories* (SAT 1); *Primetime/Spätausgabe* (*Primetime/Late Edition* – RTL); and *Zehn vor Elf* (*Ten to Eleven*, RTL)[31] – are similarly open and eclectic in their structure and encourage the audience to actively participate in the meaning-making process which is initiated but not foreclosed by the work. While each of the programs is unique in its thematic focus (topics explored include, among others, war, fascism, history, love, opera, nuclear power, neuroscience, literature, biology, philosophy, music, film, international security and economics), when viewed as a whole, they can be divided into three broad categories.

---

**29** | Ibid.
**30** | Alexander Kluge, "The Sharpest Ideology", p. 194.
**31** | A selection of Kluge's television programs has been released on DVD by the Filmmuseum München in co-operation with the Goethe Institute. The collection, which is entitled *Alexander Kluge – Arbeiten für das Fernsehen* consists of seven DVDs with subtitles in several languages, including English.

*Figure 1: 'Die Rache der betrogenen Braut' (1994)*

The first category consists of programs that seek to mobilise audience participation via a diverse montage of mixed materials that address, complicate and pose questions about the issues and ideas at hand. As per Kluge's films, these programs consist of both fictional and documentary footage (including newsreels, animation, photographs, diagrams, maps, drawings, text inserts, clips from newsreels and early cinema), much of which is encased in on-screen monitors and other framing devices such as windows, boxes and proscenium arches that break up the image and alienate the material from its original context. Stylistic devices reminiscent of early cinema (including intertitles, iris masks and colour tinting) are also employed to "reinvent the possibilities of the medium" and, in the process, to cultivate an active, creative mode of engagement via which the solidity of reality is called into question. As Kluge makes clear, his television productions are anchored "in the early experience of film [...] the first films of Méliès, of Lumière"[32] because "[i]n

---

**32** | Gertrud Koch and Heide Schlüpmann, '"Nur Trümmern trau ich...': ein Gespräch mit Alexander Kluge" in: *Kanalarbeit: Medienstrategien im Kulturwandel*, ed. Hans-Ulrich Reck, Basel and Frankfurt am Main: Stroemfeld and Roter Stern, 1998, p. 21.

each of these origins, "cousins" and other relatives of what actually developed can be found, and these can be adapted for the New Media in very interesting ways".[33]

This is not to suggest that Kluge has faith in the oft-cited claim that Lumière's work, because it provides the audience with unimpeded access to "reality", stands in marked contrast to the fantastical productions of Méliès. Rather, as the following statement makes clear, Kluge's television practice subverts the fictional/realist divide often drawn by critics to make a clear cut distinction between their work: "With the true Lumière I am with Méliès, that is reality is fiction and fiction is reality".[34]

Kluge's interest in early cinema is exemplified, for example, in "Wilde Nacht mit Mond" (Wild Night with Moon) (1990)[35]: a program that opens with footage reminiscent of a magic lantern – an early relative of the film projector. We see a black and white landscape lit, in part, by a moon located at the top right hand corner of the screen. In the other corner we are presented with footage of a tree battered by howling wind and soldiers struggling futilely in a battle landscape. This and other material reminiscent of early cinema appears in various formats throughout the course of the program and is juxtaposed with footage taken from different sources including *War and Peace* (1982) and a magic lantern depicting French soldiers participating in a parade to mark the end of the First World War.

These fragments culminate, in a sense, at the end of the program in the image of *Angelus Novus*: A painting produced by Paul Klee which served, in part, as inspiration for Walter Benjamin's "On the Concept of History" which explores the relationship between a

---

**33** | Alexander Kluge, "Why Should Film and Television Cooperate? On the Mainz Manifesto", *October*, 46 (Fall, 1988), p. 99.

**34** | "Gespräche mit Alexander Kluge", *Filmkritik*, Vol. 12 (December, 1976), p. 581.

**35** | Alexander Kluge, "Wilde Nacht mit Mond", Alexander Kluge, *Der Eiffelturm, King Kong und die weiße Frau & Mann ohne Kopf*, Edition filmmuseum 28, 2008.

conception of history driven by progress and the decline of a form of "civilisation" exemplified, in the context of the program, via images of sacrifice, horror and war. In the program's final minutes, we view the Angel of History rotating on screen wrapped in the cylindrical form of a magic lantern, while underneath moving text recounts Benjamin's analysis of the storm of progress that leaves nothing but rubble in its wake.[36]

As this example illustrates, Kluge's programs combine references to early cinema technologies that are, in part, produced by and work in conjunction with possibilities opened up by digital video including: the layering of image and text through superimposition; the production of complex collage effects created by montage within the frame; the generation and animation of digital images; an extensive use – reminiscent of Dadaist text collages – of canted words and phrases; the employment of scrolling text to pose questions and display quotes; and the magnification, duplication and fragmentation of the image. As Kluge notes in a statement that is true of both his film and television practice:

> The principle is that each [shot] has its own life. Every shot is one film. This is the way film history began. Lumiere's first film – *Repas de bébe* – is a breakfast scene with his child and wife. Behind, the branches are moving. There is a balance between the branches and the little story in the foreground. [...] So we are interested very much in short films, one minute pictures. Each has a separate life that is easy to observe. Only the convention of making extended linear narratives obscures this separate life. If you take the plot out of a conventional film the individual images become nonsense. If you take the narrative from my films, or from the films of Dovzhenko and many others, however, there will always be a beautiful garden of images. And just as in a beautiful garden, the images do not have to form a concept.

---

**36** | See Walter Benjamin's "On the Concept of History" in: Walter Benjamin, *Selected Writings: Volume 4, 1938-1940*, ed. Howard Eiland and Michael W. Jennings, Cambridge, Mass. and London, England: Harvard University Press, 2003, pp. 389-400.

You do not have to understand it; you only need to walk through it. The garden is not there to be encompassed".[37]

The mode of engagement evoked in this passage is also cultivated by the manner in which time is presented in Kluge's programs. Time lapse, for example, is extensively employed to alienate the image from its original context. As Kluge makes clear: "Time-lapse creates a totality that simultaneously changes the light we see things in, creating a new perspective on the televisually mediated event".[38] In another program – "Das Quietschen der Macht, sobald die Bremsen zieht"[39] ("The Screeching Sound of Power as Soon as it Puts on the Brakes") (1992) – this alienation effect is achieved not by manipulating the footage, but by leaving the footage intact in a manner the allows the pro-filmic material to speak for itself.

The program in question consists of footage shot at two different events: The first, the World Economic Summit held in Munich in 1992 and the latter, an economic summit in France. What is significant about the program (which aired in 1992 and which provides alternative media coverage of the Munich event) is the way in which the extended duration of the footage encourages a freedom of spectatorial movement inhibited by the carefully orchestrated form and didactic approach of television news broadcasts. The program opens with a montage of official press images of the economic summit in France. We see Boris Yeltsin, George Bush and Helmut Kohl smiling in unison and an image of political dignitaries posing in line on a stage decorated with international flags. Kluge then cuts to a still image of Goatlord (the heavy metal band whose music features in-

---

**37** | Stuart Liebman, "On New German Cinema, Art, Enlightenment", *October*, 46 (Fall, 1988), p. 54.
**38** | Astrid Deuber-Mankowsky and Giaco Schiesser, "In the Real Time of Feelings: Interview with Alexander Kluge", p. 355.
**39** | Alexander Kluge, "Das Quietschen der Macht, wenn sie die Bremsen zieht", Alexander Kluge, *Freiheit für die Konsonanten! & Grenzfälle der Schadensregulierung*, Edition filmmuseum 32, 2008.

termittently on the soundtrack) and to an intertitle in blue and white that announces the title of the program. The footage which follows focuses on the Munich event and, more specifically, on the public protests that were staged at the time. While the images that appear on screen depict scenes that may have featured in a fragmentary, clipped format in the mainstream news media, Kluge's extended presentation of protestors being man-handled by police (the opening Munich shots last, following a still image of the event, 28, 25 and 13 seconds respectively) encourage viewers not to simply register, but to reflect on and experience the complexity of the reality unfolding before them on screen.

Later in the program we view footage of a press conference in which protestors in the audience seek to vocalise their criticism of the event. In a scene that evokes the sense of futility described by Alois Becker in Kluge's story, the protestors are removed from the building and denied the opportunity to voice their critique. As a protestor is restrained by a security guard and subsequently escorted from the building, a voice over loudspeaker states: "As you can see Ladies and Gentlemen, one part of freedom is the freedom of expression for everyone" and later, "Democracy includes the freedom to shout". In contrast to television news programs which employ the voiceover of the presenter to frame and thereby shape the "meaning" of the event, Kluge allows the material to run its own course, leaving the viewer with the opportunity to interpret it for him/herself. This alienation process is also generated in scenes that follow, albeit in a different way via footage taken from *Krieg und Frieden* of the economic summit in Versailles. In this instance, however, the "civilised" images of a chamber group, soldiers and politicians eating a meal are accompanied by the loud, throbbing, monotonous tones of Goatlord's music.[40]

---

**40** | In a statement which sheds light on some of the experiential effects generated by this experimental approach, Kluge states of another program: "When we do a show like "Wir machen mit, for example, a show about the election of the Social Democratic Party Chairman in Düsseldorf, we don't

## Communicating Experience

This questioning of the status quo and the image of "reality" generated by the mainstream media is also apparent in the second category of programs that are largely interview based but which nonetheless exhibit, albeit to a lesser extent, many of the characteristics outlined above. In "Geisterstunde mit Bilder"[41], for example, we view Oskar Negt seated in a dark room in front of two monitors, both of which display black and white documentary footage of war scenes, including images of burning buildings and bomber pilots that appear to have been shot during the Second World War. In an image which evokes Negt and Kluge's analysis of the important role television *could* play in facilitating the "self-determination of [its] viewers", Negt uses the images that appear before him on the monitors as springboards for the formation of his own associations, connections and ideas. In a statement which reflects on the futility of war and, tangentially, Kluge's analysis of the degree to which televisual representations of violence and destruction anaesthetise the viewer from the images on screen, Negt states: "One doesn't know what the goal is and it also probably doesn't make any sense" (*"wahrscheinlich hat es auch kein Sinn"*).

Negt's use of the word *Sinn* is suggestive in this context insofar as it points both to the futility of war (war has no *sense*, that is, *meaning*) and to the viewer's inability to sensorially integrate such footage at the level of his/her own experience. This emphasis on the senses

---

broadcast it with audio from the party convention, which everyone's already heard in the news and current affairs shows anyway. Instead, we combine the footage with a piece of modern pop music, Last Judgement. And we show the images speeded up. Time-lapse creates a totality that simultaneously changes the light we see things in, creating a new perspective on the televisually mediated event". Astrid Deuber-Mankowsky and Giaco Schiesser, "In the Real Time of Feelings: Interview with Alexander Kluge", p. 355.

**41** | Alexander Kluge, "Geisterstunde mit Bilder", *10 vor 11* (August 27, 1990).

and on the capacity of television to "motivate feelings" is significant because, for Kluge, the task of an active public sphere is to "build streets from people to people, channels between the feelings of one person and another, in order to understand each other".[42] As Kluge makes clear, this process of understanding is generated through the cultivation of an authentic voice. "I don't believe", he states, "that viewers would bother checking the content of my programmes, which tends to be rather complicated, but they do care about the authenticity of the language: they are these real human beings who are reporting to them. And that's what sticks in the mind".[43]

Figure 2: 'Das Halten von Totenschädeln liegt mir nicht!' (2001)

In Kluge's interviews (which are shot either in public spaces such as bars, cafés, theatres, museums or, alternatively, in the private space of his Munich office) this "authentic" voice is cultivated and

---

**42** | Kluge, Alexandra and Rainer Frey, "Interview mit Alexander Kluge: Eine realistische Haltung müßte der Zuschauer haben, müßte ich haben, müßte der Film haben", *Filmfaust* 20 (November 1980), p. 24.
**43** | Astrid Deuber-Mankowsky and Giaco Schiesser, "In the Real Time of Feelings: Interview with Alexander Kluge", p. 355.

communicated in a number of ways. For example, in interviews with witnesses of the Chernobyl disaster, Kluge's aim is to provide a space within which viewers can communicate their experiences to the viewer directly. As he states in *Die Wächter des Sarkophags* (a book which contains transcripts of the programs in question): "The following documentation contains interviews that were conducted with people who had something directly to do with Chernobyl, that is people who report on direct experience".[44]

In one such interview[45], we view Oxana Pentak, an Engineer who was living and working in Pripjet at the time who recounts her experiences in the minutes, hours and days following the explosion. The interview opens with Pentak describing the night in which she and her family were woken by the event. "How", Kluge asks, "did this explosion sound?" It was, she states, "a very loud explosion. It sounded like in a war film". She then proceeds to describe the view from her ninth floor apartment: "The windows", she recalls, "faced the power station. We could see the power station. Then I saw a flame and a huge cloud of steam rise into the air". In another interview[46], this time with journalist Igor Kostin, the audience is presented with his direct, straightforward account of the event. In an interview which foregrounds the role the senses play in both enabling and communicating experience, Kostin describes what he saw, how he felt, the sensation on his skin, and the taste in his mouth when he photographed the reactor on the day following the explosion.

---

**44** | Alexander Kluge, "Einleitung" in: Alxexander Kluge, *Die Wächter des Sarkophags. 10 Jahre Tschernobyl*, Hamburg: Rotbuch-Verlag, 1996, p. 16.

**45** | Alexander Kluge, "Der Wind, der reinigt das – " ("The Wind Will Clean it Off") (1996), Alexander Kluge, *Im Rausch der Arbeit & Abschied von der sicheren Seite des Lebens* (2008).

**46** | Alexander Kluge, "Abschied von der sicheren Seite des Lebens" (A Farewell to the Secure Side of Life") (2002), Alexander Kluge, *Im Rausch der Arbeit & Abschied von der sicheren Seite des Lebens*, Edition filmmuseum 29, 2008.

*Figure 3:* 'Der Wind, der reinigt das –'

A sensorially charged mode of engagement is also facilitated, albeit in a different way, in "Die Guillotine oder die Kategorie der Plötzlichkeit"[47] ("The Guillotine or the Category of Suddenness") (1988) – a program in which Karl-Heinz Bohrer reports on the history of the Guillotine. In the opening minutes of the program, Bohrer responds to Kluge's question – "What does a Guillotine look like?" – in an emotionally neutral, somewhat scientific tone. "It is", he states,

a wooden frame which has an opening through which the offender's head is placed, and a sharp iron blade above which drops in free-fall. And the process takes place between these wooden blocks: the striking of the iron blade into the opening of the wooden section intended for the head.

In contrast to the interviews about Chernobyl described above – in which the interviewees communicate a *sense* of their experience to the audience by describing what they saw, what they tasted, what

---

**47** | Alexander Kluge, "Die Guillotine oder die Kategorie der Plötzlichkeit", Alexander Kluge, Alexander Kluge, *Der Eiffelturm, King Kong und die weiße Frau & Mann ohne Kopf*, Edition filmmuseum 28, 2008.

they heard, and what they felt – Bohrer refrains from expressing his feelings about how – and with what effects – the guillotine actually functions. Rather, in a similar vein to the open, interrupted form of the Munich footage described in the previous section, Bohrer's expert, detached tone prompts feeling in the audience because, instead of directing the viewer's thinking, his neutrality encourages the audience to imagine the device for themselves and, in the process, to think through and to *feel* the barbaric nature of such an invention.

In other cases this interactive process is facilitated by the dynamic way in which Kluge engages the interviewee in conversations that zig zag across diverse terrain while addressing the complexity of the topic in question. For example, in an interview with evolutionary biologist Peter Hammerstein in "Zauberwelt der Evolution" ("The Magical World of Evolution") (2007)[48], a conversation about the cooperative behaviour of social insects spirals into an analysis of conflict situations and the competitive drive exhibited by human beings. The discussion then refracts intuitively into a range of different topics including, among others: the territorial behaviour exhibited by chimpanzees; *Romeo and Juliet*; the politics of arranged marriages; and the secret life of genes – the functioning of which Hammerstein evocatively likens to "organ pipes" that "become active when certain keys are pressed". "[O]n your inner organs", he notes, "there is some serious playing going on".

The intuitively organised, rhizomatic structure of Kluge's programs is also demonstrated in "Was heißt 'guter Wille'?"[49] ("What does 'Good Will' mean'"?) (2007) in which Kant expert Beatrice Longuenesse talks about love, morality, and the subject/object distinction in the philosopher's work – a train of thought which leads

---

**48** | Alexander Kluge, "Zauberwelt der Evolution", Alexander Kluge, *Krieg ist das Ende aller Pläne & Woher wir kommen, wohin wir gehen*, Edition filmmuseum 31, 2008.

**49** | Alexander Kluge, "Was heißt 'guter Wille'?", Alexander Kluge, *Die poetische Kraft der Theorie & Alle Gefühle glauben an einen glücklichen Ausgang*, Edition filmmuseum 34, 2009.

her to reflect, contra Kant, on the extent to which the body is present "in the thought of the subject". Longuenesse's comments on this topic are then constellated with an intertitle in red, white and black which states "Gegenwärtigkeit des Körpers im Gedanken" ("presence of the body in thinking"): a thought which prompts Kluge to recount a story about a bomber pilot who is preparing to attack a suspected "terrorist hideout"; the location of which, unbeknown to him, is the site of a civilian wedding party. In the moment of the attack, Kluge explains, the pilot experiences an acute case of diarrhoea – a condition brought on, perhaps, by his inkling that something isn't quite right. After soiling his combat suit, he is engulfed by a sense of shame, swerves the plane, and "the projectiles land in the swamp", sparing the lives of the people who had been celebrating there. "His intestines", Kluge states, "are smarter than his common sense" – an observation which leads Longuenesse to reflect on the role that feelings and emotions play in Kant's conception of practical reasoning.[50]

## FACTS AND FAKES

The capacity to draw distinctions based on both instinct and experience is, in "Das Weichziel ist der Mensch"[51] ("Man is the Soft Target") (2008) not illustrated but set in play via the mode of en-

---

**50** | Kluge has discussed this and other related stories about bomber pilots in a range of different contexts. See, for example, "Absichtloses Glück: Eine Übersprunghandlung" in: Alexander Kluge, *Die Lücke, die der Teufel läßt: Im Umfeld des neuen Jahrhunderts*, pp. 709-711, Alexander Kluge, "Risse", *Frankfurter Allgemeine Sonntagszeitung*, October 26 (2003),p. 23 and Florian Hopf, "'Feelings Can Move Mountains: An Interview with Alexander Kluge on the Film *The Power of Feelings*" in: *Alexander Kluge: Raw Materials For the Imagination*, pp. 244-245.
**51** | Alexander Kluge, "Das Weichziel ist der Mensch" ("Man is the Soft Target") (2008), *Freiheit für die Konsonanten! & Grenzfälle der Schadensregulierung*, Edition filmmuseum 32, 2008.

gagement facilitated by the format of the interview around which the program is based. This and other programs in this category feature actors performing in the guise of interviewees and combine what Kluge describes as "facts and fakes" to destabilise the reality effects generated by the authoritative tone of the mainstream news media. While some of these programs employ comedy to render the performative nature of the interview explicit, others rely on a form of blank parody to facilitate a mode of engagement that, for Kluge, is synonymous with "criticism". "Criticism", he writes, "is the positive capacity to draw distinctions, it confirms something, it affirms something new".[52]

In "Man is the Soft Target", this blank parody is enacted by Lieutenant Colonel Sanftleben (George Schram) – a senior member of the German Bundeswehr who waxes lyrical about the benefits of long distance weapons that allow soldiers to kill the enemy "without getting splattered with blood". In a statement that reveals him to be at odds with his name ("Sanftleben" means "gentle life" in German), he states that this new technology "makes the act of killing much normal and easier for the soldier". In Sanftleben's account (which is interspersed with documentary footage of a contemporary military drill, photographs of Hitler and his generals, and Fascist propaganda) the logic and horror of war are revealed without PR filters. Anodyne terms such as "collateral damage", "soft target" and "friendly fire" are replaced with words such as "killing", "blood" and "raging pain" – all of which are expressed in a matter-of-fact, rather than a provocative or emotive style.

---

[52] | See Alexander Kluge and Joseph Vogl, "Kritik aus nächster Nähe" in: Alexander Kluge and Joseph Vogl, *Soll und Haben: Fernsehgespräche*, Zürich and Berlin: diaphenes, 2009, p. 12.

*Figure 4: 'Das Weichziel ist der Mensch'*

What is effective about this mode of communication is the way in which the upbeat, unambiguous nature of his tone destabilises – in a manner that may at first glance seem paradoxical – an unambiguous image of war rendered palatable by the mainstream news media. That is to say, although Colonel Sanftleben is played, in this instance, by an actor who is performing a role, he speaks about war in an "authentic" voice insofar as his positive, straightforward tone prompts the viewer to reflect on the contradictions inherent in a "civilised" culture in which the horror of war is framed in anodyne terms.

What is significant about Kluge's employment of fictional characters in relation to real political events is the degree to which this mixing of "fact and fake" opens up a space within which the "realism of the senses can exert a practical critique" of the reality principle governing the political sphere. Critique, in this sense, is not associated with a self-contained, autonomous form of logic that one pins onto something else. Rather, as Alois Becker makes clear in Kluge's story, critique is connected with the generation of an active public sphere within which thought processes pertaining to ideas and events are brought into contact with "human experience". "I feel pathos", Kluge writes, "at the thought, that feelings and objectivity, feelings and labour power, come together. They could, so to speak, shake up the peace."[53]

---

[53] Alexander Kluge, "Text der Pressekonferenz mit Alexander Kluge über *Die Macht der Gefühle* in Venedig am 5. September 1983", Kinemathek, 20 (September, 1983). p. 5.

# CHAPTER 3
Mobilising the Public Sphere:
Schlingensief's Reality Theatre

Christoph Schlingensief's work spans a diverse range of fields including film, theatre, art, radio, activism, opera and television.[1] His capacity to cross boundaries – not only between different media, but between art and politics, performance and reality, the private and public spheres – is reflected in the fact that he was an experimental artist who became a household name in Germany. Although he gained a certain notoriety for his film, theatre, and performance work (he was arrested, for example, during a 1997 performance at Documenta after displaying a sign that stated "Kill Helmut Kohl"[2]), it was via his work as the host of a series of television talk shows that his public profile in Germany was cemented.

The first of these programs, *Talk 2000*, is an eight-part series that was shot in 1997 and that features Schlingensief and his guests on a rotating stage in the Volksbühne canteen in Berlin. Although

---

[1] | For an overview of Schlingensief's career, see Tara Forrest and Anna Teresa Scheer ed., *Christoph Schlingensief: Art Without Borders*, Bristol and Chicago: Intellect, 2010, Pia Janke and Teresa Kovacs ed., *Der Gesamtkünstler. Christoph* Schlingensief, Wien: Praesens, 2011, and Klaus Biesenbach, Anna-Catharina Gebbers, Aino Laberenz, Susanne Pfeffer ed., *Christoph Schlingensief*, London, Koenig Books, 2013.

[2] | Helmut Kohl was the German Chancellor at the time and the title of the performance (following Joseph Beuys) was *Mein Filz, mein Fett, mein Hase!* (My felt, my fat, my hare!).

the program mimics, to a certain extent, the standardized format of television talk shows (Schlingensief interviews guests who are seated on a couch, there is a band and a studio audience), the random nature of Schlingensief's questions, his predilection for discussing issues he was experiencing at the time[3], the uncomfortable silences that ensue when he is unsure how to proceed, and his scuffles with members of the audience ensure that the program is anything but conventional.[4]

*Figure 1: U3000*

Equally unconventional is the eight-part series *U3000* which aired on MTV three years later: a talk show that was shot in a frenetic

---

**3** | This predilection is also apparent in *Die Piloten* (*The Pilots*): a series of pilot episodes for a talk show that was shot in 2007 at the Akademie der Künste in Berlin. As evidenced in Cordula Kablitz-Post's film documentation of the program entitled *Christoph Schlingensief – Die Piloten* (2009).

**4** | The series, which originally screened on SAT 1, RTL, Kanal 4, and ORF, has also been released on DVD. See Cordula Kablitz-Post (director), *Talk 2000* (2009).

fashion in Berlin's underground railway network. Located on a moving train, the program follows Schlingensief as he travels between the carriages interviewing an eclectic cohort of guests. The carriages themselves are packed to the brim with the "studio" audience, the production crew, and the over-the-top presence of Schlingensief himself, whose increasingly frenzied, discombobulated behaviour transforms the talk show into something reminiscent of a happening or experimental performance event.

Schlingensief's interest, as demonstrated by these examples, in producing television programs that are both modelled on – and transgress the boundaries of – standardised television formats became more focused in proceeding years as exemplified by three works he produced in the first years of the twenty-first century: *Bitte Liebt Österreich: Erste österreichische Koalitionswoche. (Please Love Austria: First Austrian Coalition Week)* (2000), *Freakstars 3000* (2002), and *Quiz 3000: Du bist die Katastrophe! (Quiz 3000: You are the Catastrophe!)* (2002). As I will explore in more detail in the following chapters, each of these productions is closely modelled on a reality television format that was popular in Germany at the time, and each has been transformed by Schlingensief in a manner that cultivates an active, participatory mode of engagement. I will argue that the interactive dimensions of this spectatorial relationship not only exceed those promised by the reality formats upon which Schlingensief's experiments are based (where audience participation is largely limited to the viewer's capacity to vote for or against a particular contestant), but that they generate what Alexander Kluge describes as an active public sphere; that is, an inclusive, dynamic, and collaborative space where viewers participate in debating, shaping, complicating and contesting the limited, partisan images of reality propagated by the mainstream media.[5]

---

**5** | For Kluge's thoughts on Schlingensief's work, see Alexander Kluge, "Foreword" in *Christoph Schlingensief: Art Without Borders*, pp. 1-4. Schlingensief also regularly featured on Kluge's television programs. See, for example, Alexander Kluge, "Das Halten von Totenschädeln liegt mir nicht!", Alexander

## BITTE LIEBT ÖSTERREICH

*Bitte Liebt Österreich* is the first of three reality productions explored in this book: a week-long multimedia/performance event that was staged as part of the Vienna Festwochen in June 2000 and that was closely modelled on the *Big Brother* television series that had attracted large audiences in Germany in previous months[6]. In keeping with the *Big Brother* format (in which the activities of contestants locked inside a compound are monitored on a twenty-four hour basis) Schlingensief installed a series of shipping containers in the Herbert-von-Karajan Platz in central Vienna that served as a temporary dwelling for twelve asylum seekers/contestants from Iran, Iraq, China, Zimbabwe, Kosovo, Kurdistan, Nigeria, Sri Lanka, Cameroon and Albania.[7] The activities of the contestants could be

---

Kluge, *Freiheit für die Konsonanten! & Grenzfälle der Schadensregulierung*, Edition filmmuseum 32 (2008) and Alexander Kluge, "Das Phänomen der Oper", Alexander Kluge, *Das Kraftwerk der Gefühle & Finsterlinge singen Bass*, Edition filmmuseum 33 (2008).

6 | According to Liesbet van Zoonen, the first season of *Big Brother* to air on German television (between March and June 2000) "received a unique market share of 28 percent". Moreover, she claims that the *Big Brother* web page "received an average of 3.5 million visitors a day [...] peaking at 5 million on some days, making it the most visited web site in Europe." Liesbet van Zoonen, "Desire and Resistance: *Big Brother in the Dutch Public Sphere*" in: *Big Brother International: Formats, Critics and Publics*, ed. Ernest Mathijs and Janet Jones, London and New York: Wallflower Press, 2004, p. 17. The German station which screened the program (RTL II) is also broadcast in Austria, so Austrian viewers would have been familiar with the program as well.

7 | Schlingensief claims that the container compound was not dissimilar to a real "container village" for asylum seekers that he visited in Oberhausen in 1992 during the production of his film *Terror 2000*. See Alexander Kluge and Christoph Schlingensief, "Freiheit für Alles, 1. Teil. Gespräch zwischen Alexander Kluge und Christoph Schlingensief", *Schlingensiefs Ausländer*

viewed both on-site through a series of peepholes and online via a live webcast on webfreetv.com where viewers could read more about the asylum seekers' biographies[8] and vote for their least favourite contestants.[9] At the end of each day of the event, an eviction was staged in which the two asylum seekers who had received the most votes were transferred from the compound into a black Mercedes that – according to Schlingensief who served as the "program" host – transported them across Austria's border. As I will discuss in more detail, both the evictions and the large *Ausländer Raus* (foreigners out) sign located on top of the compound generated much outcry and public debate both on the street and in the media, resulting in what Thomas Mießgang has described as "a total mobilisation of the Austrian public sphere".[10]

---

*Raus: Bitte Liebt Österreich*, ed. Matthias Lilienthal and Claus Philipp, Frankfurt am Main: Suhrkamp, 2000, p. 137.

**8** | As Elfriede Jelinek has pointed out, the asylum seekers' biographies were fictional in the sense that they were constructed out of a collection of different, albeit real, stories. See Elfriede Jelinek, "Der Raum im Raum," *Schlingensiefs Ausländer Raus: Bitte Liebt Österreich*, p. 160.

**9** | These on-site peepholes are also reminiscent of the freakshow format which Schlingensief references in his 2002 reality production *Freakstars 3000* which is discussed in the following chapter. "It was", as Robert Bogden points out, "a standard sideshow practice from the days before Barnum through the 1930s for people from the non-Western world to climb on the freak show platform to be gawked at by Americans. These non-Westerners were not necessarily individuals with disabilities, or who were unusually tall or short, or who performed some novelty act like fire eating. Such unusual people were indeed displayed; but those whose difference lay in the fact that they belonged to an unfamiliar race and culture had value as show pieces as well". See Robert Bogdan, *Freak Show: Presenting Human Oddities for Amusement and* Pleasure, Chicago: University of Chicago Press, 1988, p. 176.

**10** | Thomas Mießgang, "Im Land der Lächler. Über Jelinek, Wuttke und Schlingensief, über Salzgurken und Sachertorten: Sittenbilder aus dem Künstlerkampf gegen die neue Regierung in Wien", *Die Zeit*, 29 June, 2000:

As discussed in the previous chapter, this mobilisation process – whereby passive viewers are transformed into active participants in the political process – is a defining feature of the "expanded concept of art" that Joseph Beuys describes as "social sculpture". As Schlingensief makes clear, Beuys' work and ideas played an important role in shaping his conception of the important role that art can play in "shak[ing] up systems of thought".[11] To illustrate this point, Schlingensief recounts a story about his teenage encounter with Beuys who was invited to deliver a lecture at the Lions Club of which Schlingensief's father was a member. The audience, he notes, "fell into a collective sleep" until Beuys remarked "with a tone of utter conviction": 'I guarantee you that in seven years this social system will be completely destroyed'". What interested Schlingensief about this statement was the degree to which it had a lasting effect on his father who marked the seven year date on his calendar and reflected, over the coming years, whether change would indeed eventuate. "It was then", Schlingensief states, "that I first understood that this appearance by Beuys was basically a brilliant artwork because it got the people, at least my father, moving, to reflect on life and to face their fears"[12], "to become internally active and engaged".[13]

---

http://www.zeit.de/2000/27/200027.jelinek.xml Last accessed 8 February, 2015.

**11** | Paul Poet (director), *Ausländer Raus. Schlingensiefs Container* (2005). For Schlingensief's comments on social sculpture, see Christoph Schlingensief, *Ich weiß, ich war's*, ed. Aino Laberenz, Köln: Kiepenheuer & Witsch, 2012, p. 175. For further detail on some of the key intersections between the work of Beuys and Schlingensief, see Andreas Kotte ed., *Theater im Kasten: Rimini Protokoll – Castorfs Video – Beuys & Schlingensief – Lars von Trier*, Zürich: Chronos, 2007 and Kaspar Mühlemann, *Christoph Schlingensief und seine Auseinandersetzung mit Joseph Beuys*, Frankfurt am Main: Peter Lang, 2011.

**12** | Christoph Schlingensief, *Ich weiß, ich war's*, pp. 112-13.

**13** | Shelly Sacks, "Foreword" in: *What is Art? Conversation with Joseph Beuys*, ed. Volker Harlan, Forest Row: Claireville, 2004, p. x.

Art, in this sense, is thus not something that one "views" in a gallery or a museum and which is removed or stands apart from the world inhabited by the people who contemplate it. Rather, as will become clear, the "expanded concept of art" enacted by *Bitte Liebt Österreich* is driven by an attempt to break down the distinction between art and the everyday lives of the people who engage with it.[14] It is motivated not by a desire to direct, explain or close down meaning, but to mobilise thinking, discussion and debate and, in the process, to lay the ground via which meaningful political engagement is enabled.[15]

## POLITICAL CONTEXT

As Schlingensief has made clear, the impetus for the production was the establishment of a coalition government in Austria between Wolfgang Schüssel's conservative Austrian People's Party (ÖVP) and Jörg Haider's Freedom Party of Austria (FPÖ), the latter of which had gained an international reputation for its far-right, anti-immigration policies.[16] The furore that followed (both within and outside of Austria) was due, in large part, to the reputation that the FPÖ had developed as a party that was not only xenophobic and opposed to

---

14 | "Art", Schlingensief notes, "is only interesting for me if it is applied to life, if it scratches away at the separation between art and life". Schlingensief, *Ich weiß, ich war's*, p. 51.
15 | "I have", Beuys notes, "done certain experiments and explorations that have stimulated discussion. They were, in fact, only successful once they provoked discussion. [...] My concern can only be whether one can instigate this kind of process, this movement; in other words, whether one can bring people to and into this kind of movement, in the culture that holds and has held sway, and has numbed them into inaction". See "Conversation with Joseph Beuys: What is Art?", p. 16.
16 | See the interviews with Schlingensief about the event contained in *Schlingensief's Ausländer Raus. Bitte Liebt Österreich*.

immigration but also apologetic about Austria's involvement with and support of the Nazis during the Second World War. In fact, as Ruth Wodak and Anton Pelinka have pointed out, one of the anti-immigration slogans which featured heavily in the FPÖ's election campaign – "Stop the over-foreignisation" *(Stop der Überfremdung)* – was actually "coined by the Nazis and used by Goebbels in 1933."[17]

Both during and in the years preceding the election campaign, the so-called dangers of "over-foreignization" were driven home by the FPÖ's emphasis on the perceived connections between immigration and rising levels of crime and unemployment. On the so-called relationship between immigration and crime, Haider has stated of Vienna's Leopoldstadt district that "every second criminal offence there is committed by a foreigner"[18], while the perceived connection between immigration and unemployment has been stated by Haider in no uncertain terms: "In Austria there are 300,000 people who are unemployed and 300,000 official foreigners"[19] – a statement that suggests that if there were no "foreigners" living in Austria, all Austrians would be fully employed. According to Haider, the dangers associated with "over-foreignization" are magnified when one considers the "fact that foreigners naturally have more children"[20] – the implication being that the so-called increase in crime and unemployment levels is only going to escalate exponentially.

As these comments suggest, the image of multiculturalism propagated by Haider and the FPÖ is one of a "nightmare"[21] that is spinning out of control. "In truth", Haider has claimed, "the multi-

---

17 | Ruth Wodak and Anton Pelinka, "Introduction" in: *The Haider Phenomenon in Austria*, ed. Ruth Wodak and Anton Pelinka, New Brunswick and London: Transaction Publishers, 2002, p. xv.
18 | Haider quoted in: Hubertus Czernin ed., *Wofür ich mich meinetwegen entschuldige. Haider, beim Wort genommen*, Wien: Czernin Verlag, 2000, p. 76.
19 | Ibid., p. 87.
20 | Ibid., p. 94.
21 | Ibid., p. 81.

cultural ideology is an instrument of the left, above all in Germany, in order to instrumentalize its pathological self-hatred against its own people"[22] – a statement that is telling in the way it seeks to distinguish the FPÖ from those on the left who have sought to confront the legacy of the Nazi past in Germany. As mentioned previously, the FPÖ is infamous for the apologetic way in which it has dealt with Austria's support of and collaboration with the Nazis. Haider, in particular, has explicitly stated his support for those Austrians who worked with the Waffen SS which was "condemned as a criminal organization at the Nuremberg Trials".[23] As Lutz Musner has argued:

Haider became notoriously well-known for such remarks as in September 1995, when he addressed an annual meeting of former SS officers at Ulrichsberg in Carinthia with the statement, 'The Waffen SS was a part of the Wehrmacht and hence it deserves all the honor and respect of the army in public life.' He then went on to characterize the nostalgia-driven SS veterans who gather every year to recycle their Nazi memories as 'people of good character who also stick to their convictions, despite the greatest opposition and have remained true to their convictions until today'.[24]

Such comments have been greeted with much criticism and, in fact, after praising the employment policies of the Third Reich in 1991, Haider was forced to resign from his then position of Governor of Carinthia.[25] Nonetheless, Haider and the FPÖ have received much public support from the media, and from Austria's largest tabloid newspaper, the *Kronen Zeitung*, in particular, which has actively sup-

---

22 | Ibid., p. 83.
23 | Walter Manoschek, "FPÖ, ÖVP, and Austria's Nazi Past" in Wodak and Pelinka ed., *The Haider Phenomenon in Austria*, p. 8.
24 | Lutz Musner, "Memory and Globalization: Austria's Recycling of the Nazi Past and its European Echoes", *New German Critique*, No. 80 (Spring-Summer 2000), p. 79.
25 | Ibid.

ported both the FPÖ's anti-immigration policies and its apologetic take on Austria's involvement with the Nazis.[26]

What is important to point out, particularly in the context of this chapter, is that the FPÖ has also been active in seeking to both discredit and remove public funding for those artists, writers and theatre practitioners who espouse ideas and concerns that are seen as inimical to the party's own. As Andre Gingrich has discussed in some detail, in 1995 the FPÖ staged a poster campaign that directly targeted artists and writers (including Elfriede Jelinek and Thomas Bernhard) whom they describe as "defamers of Austria".[27] As Haider has stated publicly on a number of occasions: "We won't allow the slandering of Austria, if it is practiced by subsidized writers. [...] The FPÖ won't allow our beautiful homeland to be smeared"[28]. As Gingrich has pointed out, these campaigns were staged to appeal to those "who are interested primarily or exclusively in mass entertainment and popular art". By appealing to the interests of this particular constituency, he argues that the FPÖ was able to successfully generate "an artificial rupture between popular culture and 'serious' art, aligning the latter with radicals and intellectuals and re-orienting popular culture along neo-conservative and neo-nationalist lines".[29]

What is particularly interesting about Schlingensief's work in this context is the way in which he has frequently drawn on popular cultural forms (including television talk shows and reality programs

---

26 | For a detailed analysis of the important role that the *Kronen Zeitung* has played in supporting Haider and the FPÖ, see David Art, *The Politics of the Nazi Past in Germany and Austria*, New York: Cambridge University Press, 2006, pp. 188-191.

27 | Andre Gingrich, "A Man for All Seasons: An Anthropological Perspective on Public Representation and Cultural Politics of the Austrian Freedom Party", in Wodak and Pelinka eds., *The Haider Phenomenon in Austria*, p. 83.

28 | Haider quoted in Czernin ed., *Wofür ich mich meinetwegen entschuldige*, p. 99.

29 | Andre Gingrich, "A Man for All Seasons", pp. 84-5.

such as singing contests and quiz shows[30]) in an attempt to mobilize public debate about contemporary politics. More specifically, Schlingensief's decision to model *Bitte Liebt Österreich* on the *Big Brother* format was highly effective in the Austrian (and broader European) context, not only because of the extent to which it simultaneously affirmed *and* disrupted Haider's alignment of popular culture with neo-conservative politics, but because of the way in which the *Big Brother* format enabled him to tap into the large audience base that the television series had secured across Europe at the time.

Interestingly, the format of the *Big Brother* television program (which was developed in the late 1990s by Dutch producer John de Mol) has itself been credited, in some of the many countries in which it has been produced and shown, with sparking public debate about a diverse range of issues. For example, in his discussion of the 2003 series of *Big Brother* Africa (which was "the highest-rated television programme in the history of African television") Daniël Biltereyst claims that the program was praised for drawing public attention to the AIDS crisis in Africa.[31] During the 2007 UK series of *Celebrity Big Brother*, the racist behaviour exhibited by some housemates toward Indian actress and co-housemate Shilpa Shetty sparked thousands of viewer complaints, protests in India, as well as public debate about racism in Britain, while in the 2004 series of *Big Brother* Australia, housemate Merlin Luck took advantage of the live eviction show to draw public attention to the plight of asylum seekers incarcerated in detention centres by the conservative Howard government. Wearing tape across his mouth, and holding a sign that stated "Free th[e] Refugees", Luck claimed that his aim had

---

**30** | Two of these productions – *Freakstars 3000* (a singing contest) and *Quiz 3000* (a quiz show) – will be discussed in Chapters 5 and 6 respectively.
**31** | Daniel Biltereyst, "*Big Brother* and Its Moral Guardians: Reappraising the Role of Intellectuals in the *Big Brother* Panic", in: *Big Brother International: Formats, Critics and Publics*, pp. 9-10.

been to stage a silent protest in an attempt to put the "issue [of mandatory detention for asylum seekers] back on the political agenda".³²

Figure 2: Bitte Liebt Österreich

What was, however, particularly effective about Schlingensief's employment of the *Big Brother* format to mobilize public debate about the anti-immigration policies of the FPÖ was his transformation of the *Big Brother* house into a temporary dwelling for asylum seekers; the structure of which, Schlingensief claims, was not dissimilar to a real "container village" for asylum seekers that he visited in Oberhausen in 1992 during the production of his film *Terror 2000* (1992).³³ The

---

32 | Merlin Luck quoted in: Anonymous, "Merlin breaks silence on *Big Brother* protest", *Sydney Morning Herald*, 14 June, 2004: http://www.smh.com.au/articles/2004/06/14/1087065072743.html Last accessed 8 February, 2014.

33 | Alexander Kluge and Christoph Schlingensief, "Freiheit für Alles, 1. Teil. Gespräch zwischen Alexander Kluge und Christoph Schlingensief" in: *Schlingensiefs Ausländer Raus*, p. 137.

image of the "Ausländer Raus" sign towering over a compound encircled by security guards and metal fences also functioned to evoke images of the concentration camps run by the Nazis – a connection that was made explicit in the original title of the performance: *Bitte Liebt Österreich: Erste europäische Konzentrationswoche (Please love Austria: First European Concentration Week)*, the subtitle of which was subsequently replaced with *Erste europäische Koalitionswoche (First European Coalition Week)*.[34]

## PLAYING OUT POLITICS

Schlingensief's decision to model *Bitte Liebt Österreich* on the *Big Brother* format grew, as per Beuys' delineation of the task of social sculpture, out of a desire to maximize the audience's interaction with the issues and concerns raised by the performance. Schlingensief claims that what troubles him, in particular, about much contemporary theatre is the lack of exchange between the audience and the issues and ideas presented on stage:

these lying machines bore me in the theatre, where ideas can't really be grasped, only in an abstract setting: the viewer sits in front of them, the director sits, in the meantime, in a bus or an aeroplane and speeds towards the next idea. [...] For me, that isn't a process of exchange.[35]

---

34 | For a discussion of the reasons for this change, see Anonymous, "Keine Wiener 'Konzentrationswoche'", *Die Presse*, 7 June 2000.
35 | Stefan Lätzer and Jakob Buhre, "Die Ursache liegt in der Zukunft", *Planet Interview*, 27 February, 2001: http://www.planet-interview.de/interviews/pi.php?interview=Schlingensief-christoph Last accessed 8 February, 2015. See also Schlingensief's discussion of the cool, distant spectatorial relationship cultivated by such performance practices in Schlingensief, "Wir sind zwar nicht gut, aber wir sind da" in: Julia Lochte and Wilfried Schulz eds., *Schlingensief! Notruf für Deutschland. Über die Mission, das Theater*

In the case of *Bitte Liebt Österreich*, Schlingensief has sought – on a number of different levels – to actively cultivate a process of exchange between the audience and the ideas and concerns raised by the performance; the most obvious (and perhaps least productive) of which could be seen in the audience's capacity to vote online for their least-favourite asylum seeker. A much more interesting, and certainly more significant process of exchange was, however, prompted by the ambiguity surrounding the performance itself, and the fact that it was very unclear who was actually responsible for staging the event; an ambiguity that prompted the audience to actively participate in the meaning-making process that was initiated, but not directly circumscribed by the people, images, slogans and ideas with which they came into contact.

In keeping with Beuys' non-pedagogical approach, Schlingensief has stated in an interview with Kluge that his aim was not to produce a "pedagogical event"[36]. That is to say, his intention was not to actively criticise the FPÖ (and thereby inform the audience, in a didactic fashion, about the dangers their policies represent). In contrast to claims by Heidemarie Unterrainer (the cultural spokesperson for the FPÖ) that Schlingensief had actively sought to produce "images of Austria that damage Austria's reputation"[37], Schlingensief claims that his aim was simply to engage with the FPÖ on its own terms. "We produce images", he states, "that simply take Haider and his slogans at their word"[38]. "I take Haider-lines and I

---

*und die Welt des Christoph Schlingensief*, Hamburg: Rotbuch Verlag, 1998, p. 22.

**36** | Alexander Kluge, "Theater der Handgreiflichkeit/Christoph Schlingensiefs Wiener Container", *News and Stories*, SAT 1, October 22, 2000.

**37** | Heidemarie Unterrainer in Paul Poet (director), *Ausländer Raus. Schlingensiefs Container* (2005).

**38** | Verbatim transcription of comments made by Schlingensief during a television debate about the event: "*Zeit im Bild 3*, ORF, 13. 6. 2000" in: Lilienthal and Philipp ed., *Schlingensiefs Ausländer Raus*, p. 99.

simply say: 'I'm playing out Haider'. That was the basic idea of this container".³⁹

This "playing out" of the FPÖ (what Schlingensief, in another context, has described as a process of "recapitulation"⁴⁰) was enacted by *Bitte Liebt Österreich* on a number of different levels. For example, the container compound itself was plastered with FPÖ slogans such as *"Stop der Überfremdung"*, *"Wien darf nicht Chicago werden"* ("Vienna must not become Chicago"), and *"Unsere Ehre heisst Treue"* ("Our honour is loyalty") – the latter of which was the "oath of allegiance of the Waffen-SS" that was publicly reiterated in 2000, in gratitude to his supporters, by then chairman of the FPÖ Ernest Windholz.⁴¹ Throughout the seven-day performance, FPÖ flags

---

**39** | Kluge, "Theater der Handgreiflichkeit/Christoph Schlingensiefs Wiener Container". As Burghart Schmidt makes clear in his analysis of Schlingensief's strategy in this regard: "You don't need to comment to articulate criticism. It is simply enough to cite what you criticise. The quotes just need to be placed in the right position at the right time and place. Then suddenly a simple citation becomes self-revelatory". Paul Poet (director), *Ausländer Raus. Schlingensiefs Container*, 2005. See also Schlingensief's discussion of this practice in *Ich weiß, ich war's*, p. 95.

**40** | Kluge,"Theater der Handgreiflichkeit/Christoph Schlingensiefs Wiener Container". In their brief analysis of *Bitte Liebt Österreich* in the context of works produced by other artists, Inke Arns and Sylvia Sasse describe this recapitulation process as a form of "subversive affirmation", that is: "an artistic/political tactic that allows artists/activists to take part in certain social, political, or economic discourses and affirm, appropriate or consume them while simultaneously undermining them. It is characterised precisely by the fact that with affirmation simultaneously there is taking place a distancing to, or revelation of what is being affirmed. In subversive affirmation there is always a surplus which destabilizes affirmation and turns it into its opposite". See Inka Arns and Sylvia Sasse, "Subversive Affirmation: On Mimesis as a Strategy of Resistance" in: IRWIN (ed.), *East Art Map: Contemporary Art and Eastern Europe*, London: Afterall, 2006, p. 445.

**41** | Manoschek, "FPÖ, ÖVP, and Austria's Nazi Past", p. 6.

were displayed on the containers, recordings of Haider's voice could be heard over loudspeaker announcing that Austria "has reached its maximum limit, we can't take any more [immigrants]"[42], and Schlingensief moved around the compound and addressed the large crowds with statements such as: "This is the truth, this is the FPÖ, this is the *Kronen Zeitung*, this is Austria"[43]. Instigating a process he described as "image disruption"[44], Schlingensief implored tourists who had gathered around the container to "take a photo, send it to your homeland and write on the back: This is Austria"[45]

Such statements, however, only added to the confusion experienced by both tourists and locals alike because, as stated previously, it wasn't clear who was responsible for staging the event.[46] Indeed, given the FPÖ's very public alignment of popular culture with

---

42 | Helmut Schödel, "Die Indianer von Wien", *Schlingensiefs Ausländer Raus: Bitte Liebt Österreich*, ed. Matthias Lilienthal and Claus Philipp, p. 173. A number of these broadcasts are audible on the soundtrack of *Ausländer Raus* including, for example, the following statement: "We also believe", Haider declares, that "those hundred thousand illegal aliens in this country carry no right to remain in this country! Therefore they have to leave this land by our will, if they are proven delinquents! Cause we don't want to breed crime".

43 | Paul Poet, *Ausländer Raus. Schlingensiefs Container*.

44 | As Schlingensief has stated of the production: "I wanted to build "a machine that disrupts images". Christoph Schlingensief, *Ich weiß, ich war's*, p. 105. For an analysis of this concept in relation to Schlingensief's work, see Lars Koch, "Christoph Schlingensief's Bilderstörungsmashine", *Zeitschrift für Literaturwissenschaft und Linguistik*, 44, 173 (2014).

45 | Schlingensief quoted in Karin Cerny, "Wien, erster Tag", *Berliner Zeitung* (14 June 2000).

46 | As Carl Hegemann has stated of the sense of ambiguity generated by *Bitte Liebt Österreich:* "This is what links all Schlingensiefs actions together. They invent situations that admit no clear understanding. You can't really judge for yourself what is happening here". See Paul Poet, *Ausländer Raus. Schlingensiefs Container*.

conservative politics, and given the various FPÖ slogans displayed during the event, *Bitte Liebt Österreich* appeared to have been staged by the FPÖ itself – a connection that was made explicit by Schlingensief who stated on a number of occasions that he was, in fact, from the FPÖ.[47] Addressing the crowd on a megaphone in front of the containers, he claimed: "This is the new way, ladies and gentlemen. This is foreigners out! This is Vienna! This is Nazi! This is you and I! This production is presented to you by the FPÖ in association with the *Krönen Zeitung*." Over the course of the event, however, Schlingensief alternated this and similar statements with comments that were confusing and/or provocative in tone: Some, for example, were directly critical of Austria and the FPÖ ("The super stupid Austrians", he stated, "have voted a super stupid coalition! That's the way things look right at the moment"), while others were much more ambiguous ("So now we will initiate an act that is real. I'm saying it again! This is a performance of the Wiener Festwochen. This is an actor. This is the absolute truth").

As the event unfolded, this lack of distinction between what Kluge describes as "fact and fake"[48] proved to be highly effective in mobilizing spectators to actively participate in a very public debate about both the status of the performance itself and, more significantly, the xenophobic, anti-immigration policies of Haider and the FPÖ. Indeed, Kluge's description of Schlingensief as a "public sphere generator" ("Öffentlichkeitsmacher"[49]) is apt in this context, particularly when considered in light of Kluge's delineation of the relationship between an active public sphere and the kind of spectatorial effects he seeks to generate via his own experimental film and television work.

---

**47** | Schlingensief, "Containerreport (I)" in: Lilienthal and Philipp ed., *Schlingensiefs Ausländer Raus*, p. 49.

**48** | Alexander Kluge and Christoph Schlingensief, "Freiheit für Alles, 1. Teil", p. 140.

**49** | Alexander Kluge and Christoph Schlingensief, "Freiheit für Alles, 2. Teil" in: Lilienthal and Philipp ed., *Schlingensiefs Ausländer Raus*, p. 191.

To reiterate ideas discussed in the previous chapters: central to Kluge's conception of the task of a political film practice is not only the creative autonomy of the director but the active participation of the spectator. It is not his or her task, Kluge claims, to "understand" the intentions of the director, but to actively participate in the meaning-making process that is engendered but not directly circumscribed by the "raw materials" out of which the film is constructed. Film, Kluge argues, "is not produced by auteurs alone, but by the dialogue between spectators and authors"[50] – a dialogue that is not manifested in the film itself, but rather in the associations cultivated in "the spectator's head" by "the gaps [...] between the disparate elements of filmic expression".[51]

Schlingensief too places great importance on the open, ambiguous character of his work. Taking Kluge's analysis of the active mode of spectatorship cultivated by an unfinished film practice a step further, Schlingensief has stated: "I've had the idea of producing a film by me on CD-Rom, where the speech, the images and the music are separate. And each person can put it together on the computer. Each person can make their own film".[52]

Expanding on these ideas in the context of Schlingensief's desire to actively cultivate a process of exchange between the audience and the issues and ideas raised by the performance, the greater the degree of reciprocity between the audience and the ideas being "played out" on the public stage, the more effective the performance is. In a statement that recalls Kluge's delineation of "the film in the spectator's head" and the symbiotic relationship between an active, par-

---

50 | Jan Dawson, "But why are the Questions so abstract: An interview with Alexander Kluge" in: Jan Dawson, *Alexander Kluge and the Occasional Work of a Female Slave*, New York: Zoetrope, 1977, p. 37.
51 | Edgar Reitz, Alexander Kluge, and Wilfried Reinke, "Word and Film", *October*, 46 (Fall, 1988), p. 87.
52 | Schlingensief, "Wir sind zwar nicht gut, aber wir sind da", p. 35. As Schlingensief has stated in another context: "I need the unfinished". See p. 27.

ticipatory mode of engagement and a dynamic public sphere, Schlingensief describes the container compound as "an empty surface" upon which the audience was able to "project" their own film. As one journalist put it: "Everything that happens here happens in people's heads. [...] The container could just as well be empty".[53]

As revealed in Paul Poet's documentation of the event,[54] *Bitte Liebt Österreich* proved to be highly effective in mobilizing public debate both on the street and in the media, as well as via the official site on webfreetv.com, which received 80,000 hits in the first hour of the performance.[55] Throughout the duration of the event, large crowds gathered in the Herbert-von-Karajan-Platz itself to debate the policies of the FPÖ in the public realm producing – in the process – a situation that Beuys describes as "permanent conference."[56] For example, an elderly man sporting war medals emerged to vocally support the expulsion of foreigners from Austria ("We're going to

---

**53** | Thomas Rottenberg in *Schlingensiefs Ausländer Raus: Bitte Liebt Österreich*, p. 98.
**54** | Paul Poet, *Ausländer Raus. Schlingensiefs Container*.
**55** | Kluge and Schlingensief, "Freiheit für Alles, 1. Teil", p. 148.
**56** | For a discussion of this concept, see Claudia Mesch, "Institutionalizing Social Sculpture: Beuys' *Office for Direct Democracy through Referendum* Installation, 1972" in: Claudia Mesch and Viola Michely ed., *Joseph Beuys: The Reader*, Cambridge, MA.: The MIT Press, 2007. Beuys, she argues, "established a number of counter-institutional frameworks for what he termed 'permanent conference', or, for the public debate and discussion of a multitude of social and political issues. By means of these institutions and their wide-ranging discussions, Beuys would realize his theoretical system of social sculpture and the 'expanded notion of art'". p. 198. See also Shelley Sacks' analysis of the participatory, non-pedagogically driven mode of engagement characteristic of "permanent conference" and "social sculpture" in "Seeing the phenomenon and imaginal thought: Trajectories for transformation in the work of Joseph Beuys and Rudolf Steiner" in: Alison Holland ed., *Joseph Beuys and Rudolf Steiner: Imagination, Inspiration, Intuition*, Melbourne: National Gallery of Victoria, 2007, pp. 42-43.

kill 'em all! Heads off! he claimed, to which Schlingensief responded: "Yes, official executions in public!"); a middle-aged man and his children carried a sign registering their shame about the slogans displayed during the event; an angry local was arrested for trying to pull down the signs ("Who", he yelled, "are the dirty pigs authorizing this? I am an Austrian. But I am for foreigners"); the containers were attacked with fire and acid; a man in the crowd sought to reinstate the picture of Austria that Schlingensief's "image disruption machine" had sullied ("We", he yelled, "are a country of culture you know! Listen to Mozart, go to the opera"); a hacker with the name of "Recht und Ordnung" ("law and order") temporarily shut down the server; Schlingensief was berated for wasting tax payers' money; and tourists and locals alike gathered around to discuss and try to make sense of the event. As one tour guide quoted in *Die Presse* has stated of his experience of the performance:

The people are shocked, outraged and horrified when they see the "Ausländer Raus" sign' [...]. 'I then explain to them that it's a protest and that it's not real. But there are many groups, whose tour guides only come to Vienna once a month. They're then not aware of this". The Result: The tourists believe that it's a protest against foreigners that's taking place here.[57]

Others, however, questioned the status of the performance itself. "This must be a joke", one woman commented after viewing the asylum seekers through a gap in the wall while another asked in an angry, frustrated tone:: "This is art? What? This is supposed to be art?".[58]

---

**57** | Anonymous, "Die Touristen sind entsetzt und empört", *Die Presse* (15 June 2000).

**58** | See Paul Poet, *Ausländer Raus. Schlingensiefs Container.*

*Figure 3: Ausländer Raus: Schlingensiefs Container*

In the context of Schlingensief's analysis of the lack of reciprocity characteristic of much contemporary theatre, the audience's attempts to actively "make sense" of *Bitte Liebt Österreich* must be seen as an integral part of the performance itself. Indeed, Schlingensief's description of the event as a "a tangible theatre" (*"Theater der Handgreiflichkeit"*)[59] is apt in this context because it emphasises the active, "hands-on" manner in which meaning is generated via the audience's interaction with the performance. According to Schlingensief, such a theatre practice differs significantly from performances that are "refined"[60] in their structure: a term that evokes both the closed, finished character of the kind of productions that Schlingensief criticises, and the distant, polite, auratic mode of engagement he associates with them.

---

**59** | Kluge, "Theater der Handgreiflichkeit/Christoph Schlingensiefs Wiener Container".
**60** | Ibid.

In a similar vein to the unfinished, indeterminate structure characteristic of Kluge's experimental work, the sense of ambiguity both surrounding and generated by *Bitte Liebt Österreich* prompted viewers to actively participate in a process that Schlingensief describes as "self-provocation"[61]; that is to say, a process in which it is the responsibility of the viewer to both work through – and try to make sense of – the feelings, ideas, concerns and prejudices aroused in them by the event. For Kluge, this process of "self-provocation" is an integral element of what it means to actively participate in the public sphere. Because, rather than delegating the formation of public opinion to journalists and politicians (and, indeed, to theatre directors, television producers and filmmakers), spectators are, in this context, the active "producers of their own experience".[62]

## IMAGE DISRUPTION

Interestingly, for the benefit of the many tourists who gathered around the containers, and in an attempt to counteract the negative image of Austria generated by the "Ausländer Raus" sign towering over the square, Vienna's mayor Michael Häupl stationed a truck in the vicinity of the area bearing a sign that stated: "This is not reality. This is a game. A dangerous game with people's feelings.

---

**61** | Schlingensief quoted in anonymous, "Keine Wiener-'Konzentrationswoche'".

**62** | Alexander Kluge, "Pact with a dead man" in: Eric Rentschler ed., *West German Filmmakers: Visions and Voices*, New York and London: Holmes and Meier, 1998, p. 236. These ideas are discussed in more detail in Oskar Negt and Alexander Kluge, *Public Sphere and Experience: Toward an Analysis of the Bourgeois and Proletarian Public Sphere*, Minneapolis: University of Minnesota Press, 1993.

[...] Austria is different". ⁶³ While leaflets distributed to people in the area read:

A performance of the *Wiener Festwochen* is taking place here. [...] The director Christoph Schlingensief would herewith like to comment on the difficulties of the foreign asylum seeker in our industrialised and globalised society and, at the same time, to promote discussion about Austria's domestic and foreign political situation. ⁶⁴

While the Mayor's office worked actively to "explain" the event, on the fourth day of the performance a large group of anti-FPÖ activists stormed the compound shouting "Nazis out. Free the Refugees" and "1, 2, 3, let them free". After scaling the containers and defacing the "Ausländer Raus" sign with graffiti that stated "Widerstand" ("resistance") and "Kampf dem Rassismus" ("fight racism"), they entered the compound with the aim of "liberating" the asylum seekers: "We want to bring you freedom", they stated. "We are from the antifascistic front".⁶⁵ As a result of their actions (that were, ironically, undertaken in solidarity with the performance itself) the event was temporarily shut down and the asylum seekers removed from the compound to a hotel." I say "ironically" because, as Schlingensief himself has stated of the protest: "These resistance groups continue

---

**63** | Quoted in Helmut Schödel, "Die Indianer von Wien", *Schlingensiefs Ausländer Raus*, pp. 170-1.
**64** | Quoted in Helmut Schödel, "Die Ausländer-Beschwörung" in: Lilienthal and Philipp ed., *Schlingensiefs Ausländer Raus*, pp. 154-5. As Schlingensief has pointed out, in contrast to his own desire to generate ambiguity, the mayor's office wanted to "create clarity" because they "couldn't bear such a tumult". See *Ich weiß, ich wär's*, p. 99.
**65** | Quoted by Matthias Lilienthal in Poet. "Free the asylum seekers?" Schlingensief asked. "What is that supposed to mean?" See *Ich weiß, ich wär's*, p. 101.

to believe that one only has to rip down an FPÖ flag, and then the FPÖ will go away as well".⁶⁶

As one of the protestors stated in discussion with the production crew after the protest had abated, the actions of the resistance group were, in part, motivated by Schlingensief's public criticism of the fact that the government had allowed racist slogans to be displayed in the public realm. "Imagine", Schlingensief announced to the crowd: "The coalition you have voted for keeps a slogan like this in public for two and half days now. Since two and a half days the ÖVP and the FPÖ do nothing to put it away. How damn stupid this coalition must be to keep this hanging for two and a half days!"⁶⁷

In the context of Schlingensief's description of the compound as an "image disruption machine" which challenges the "wholesome" picture of Austria generated by the *Krönen Zeitung* and the FPÖ, the actions of the demonstrators (and their public defacement of the *"Ausländer Raus"* sign in particular) functioned, as one commentator has claimed, to "clean[...] Austria by destroying the reve-

---

66 | "Bürgerkrieg im Organismus. Peter Sloterdijk im Gespräch mit Christoph Schlingensief" in: *Schlingensiefs Ausländer Raus*, p. 228. For a more detailed discussion of this protest, see Helmut Schödel, "Die Indianer von Wien", pp. 170-3.

67 | Poet, *Ausländer Raus. Schlingensiefs Container*. As Schlingensief noted, however, of the government's response, or lack thereof: "No matter what they did, it could only be the wrong move. To leave the sign hanging meant to approve of the demand 'Foreigners out!'; to take it down meant to undermine a subtly expressed election campaign slogan of the Austrian Freedom Party (FPÖ), which is now in government. The party had really used the slogan". Schlingensief, "My work always has something to do with a change of perspective" (interviewed by Hans Ulrich Obrist) in: Alice Koegel and Kasper König ed., *AC: Christoph Schlingensief: Church of Fear*, Köln: Museum Ludwig and Verlag der Buchhandlung Walther König, 2005, p. 22. I have altered the English translation of "Ausländer Raus!" from "Foreigners go home!" to "Foreigners out!". See the original German text on p. 14.

latory stigmata".⁶⁸ Schlingensief too has stated something similar noting that, by "carrying out the dirty work" that should have been undertaken by the government, the protestors became a "washing machine" for the FPÖ.⁶⁹

In contrast, Schlingensief's motivation for staging the event was to make publicly explicit what was implicit in the party's policies and slogans. By "playing out" Haider and the FPÖ on the public stage, his aim was not to shut down, but to actively mobilise debate and – in doing so – to challenge viewers to become active participants in the meaning-making process that was initiated, but not foreclosed by the event. In keeping with the non-pedagogical approach advocated by both Kluge and Beuys, for Schlingensief, this mobilisation process is not facilitated by overt resistance, nor by replacing a negative image with one which is more positive in its focus. "Resistance", he states, "is over. You have to produce contradictions"⁷⁰ because it is by generating paradox and ambiguity that thinking is set into motion.

At the conclusion of the event, the relationship between this active, creative mode of engagement and a dynamic public sphere was framed in explicitly Beuysian terms. "We are all artists" Schlingensief announced to the crowd as he handed the prize money to the competition winner: Sri Lankan asylum seeker Ranil Shunta. By staging the performance outside of what he describes as the "artistic dead-end"⁷¹ of the classical theatre, Schlingensief was able to extend

---

68 | Poet, *Ausländer Raus*.
69 | *Ich weiß, ich wär's*, p. 101.
70 | Poet, *Ausländer Raus*. Arns and Sasse are similarly cynical about the critical mode of engagement facilitated by direct resistance. "Today", they write, "in a situation characterised by the immediate and total recuperation of the critical viewpoints by the dominant political and economic capitalist system, the concept of critical distance proves to be completely ineffective". Arns and Sasse, "Subversive Affirmation: On Mimesis as a Strategy of Resistance", p. 455.
71 | Schlingensief, "Wir sind zwar nicht gut, aber wir sind da", p. 12.

the reach of his work into the public realm by encouraging viewers to become active participants in the "social sculpture" initiated by the event. Moreover, by embracing the format of *Big Brother*, Schlingensief not only broadened his audience base. He demonstrated – in a very powerful fashion – the important role that a publicly accessible performance practice can play as a catalyst for political debate.

# CHAPTER 4

Productive Discord: Schlingensief, Adorno, and *Freakstars 3000*

> The world is asynchronous and I am atonal.
> I have always worked atonally.
>
> CHRISTOPH SCHLINGENSIEF[1]

In an interview with Alexander Kluge conducted in 2001, Schlingensief reflects on the degree to which he is often perceived as a prankster; someone who likes to have fun and who can't, as a result, be taken very seriously.[2] In another context, and presumably in reaction to this negative portrait generated by the media, Schlingensief discusses the critical, one-dimensional conception of fun that underpins such criticism of his work. "When", he notes,

---

[1] | Christoph Schlingensief, "My work always has something to do with a change of perspective" (interviewed by Hans Ulrich Obrist) in: *AC: Christoph Schlingensief. Church of Fear*, ed. Alice Koegel and Kasper König, Köln: Museum Ludwig and Verlag der Buchhandlung Walther König, 2005, p. 19.

[2] | Alexander Kluge, "Das Halten von Totenschädeln liegt mir nicht!/Christoph Schlingensief inszeniert Hamlet", *News & Stories*, SAT 1 (December 16, 2001). This discussion has been reproduced in Heineke and Sandra Umathum ed., *Christoph Schlingensiefs Nazis Rein*, Frankfurt am Main: Suhrkamp, 2002, p. 122. See also Schlingensief's comments in this regard quoted in Klaes Tindemans, "The Wounded German Body of Christoph Schlingensief" in: *Art and Activism in the Age of Globalization*, ed. Lieven De Cauter, Rube De Roo and Karel Vanhaesebrouck, Rotterdam: NAi, 2011, p. 117.

> I scramble about for, and in front of, other people, then of course I can't say that I'm not having fun, otherwise I wouldn't do it. But as soon as you say that, you are immediately in the Fun Factory, or in the Fun Parade or about to get an invitation to *"RTL Samstag Nacht"* [RTL Saturday Night] where you can tell another joke about Poland or homeless people. When it comes to the word "fun", everyone listens attentively and says: "Ah, a bit of fun? Do you like a bit of fun?" No, I don't like this kind of fun. Fun is not the Comedy-Show, but desire and enthusiasm for making associations and rebuilding sentences in order to keep [fun] alive. One has to transform the lack of desire to participate in life into energy for the process of searching for something that affords pleasure.[3]

Schlingensief distinguishes here between two different modes of experiencing what he interchangeably refers to as "fun" or "pleasure". The first mode – which is associated with the idea of the "fun factory" – is strongly reminiscent of the passive, alienated mode of engagement that Theodor Adorno associates with the mass-produced products of the culture industry. In Adorno's writings on popular music, television, and other forms of mass-produced culture, fun is associated with "canned" laughter, conformity, standardization, and pre-digested material that reinforces the status quo. As Adorno and Max Horkheimer write in *Dialectic of Enlightenment*: "Amusement", in this context, "congeals into boredom, since, to be amusement, it must cost no effort and therefore moves strictly along the well-worn grooves of association. The spectator must need no thoughts of his own: the product prescribes each reaction".[4]

---

**3** | Christoph Schlingensief, "Wir sind zwar nicht gut, aber wir sind da" in: *Schlingensief! Notruf für Deutschland. Über die Mission, das Theater und die Welt des Christoph Schlingensief*, Julia Lochte and Wilfried Schulz ed., Hamburg: Rotbuch Verlag, 1998, p. 19. *RTL Samstag Nacht* was a comedy sketch show that screened on RTL in Germany in the 1990s.
**4** | Max Horkheimer and Theodor W. Adorno, *Dialectic of Enlightenment: Philosophical Fragments*, Stanford: Stanford University Press, 2002, p. 109.

In his essay "On Popular Music", Adorno claims that this non-productive, non-participatory mode of having fun fostered by the entertainment industry is a "correlate" of alienated forms of mechanized labor that leave workers feeling exhausted, bored, and unfulfilled.[5] According to Adorno, because standardized forms of mass entertainment (such as popular music and television) do not require any real effort or concentration, they provide the worker with "relief from both boredom and effort simultaneously".[6] The workers, he writes, "seek novelty, but the strain and boredom associated with actual work leads to avoidance of effort in that leisure-time which offers the only chance for really new experience".[7]

In stark contrast to this alienated conception of what it means to "have fun", the second definition touched on by Schlingensief is associated with an active, creative mode of engagement: a mode in which the capacity to draw and make one's own connections and associations is absolutely central to the production and experience of pleasure. The emphasis here is not on the kind of "canned" pleasures that Adorno associates with the consumption of "premasticated material".[8] Rather, this mode of experience is bound with the capacity to actively "participate in life" and to draw on one's own

---

**5** | Adorno, Theodor W., "On Popular Music" in: *Essays on Music*, ed. R. Leppert, Berkeley and Los Angeles: University of California Press, 2002, p. 458. In his "Prologue to Television", Adorno extrapolates on this idea: "What has long since happened to the symphony, which the tired office worker tolerates with a distracted ear while sitting in shirt sleeves slurping his soup, is now overtaking images as well. They are supposed to lend lustre to his dreary quotidian life and nevertheless essentially resemble it: In this way, they are futile from the start". Theodor W. Adorno, "Prologue to Television", *Critical Models: Interventions and Catchwords*, New York: Columbia University Press, 2005, p. 52.
**6** | Adorno, "On Popular Music", p. 458.
**7** | Ibid., p. 459.
**8** | Theodor W. Adorno, *Introduction to the Sociology of Music*, New York: Continuum, 1989, p. 30.

imagination in the process of engaging creatively with the material in question.⁹

In Adorno's writings, a similarly active, creative mode of engagement is explored in his analysis of modernist art practices, and in his essays on the work of Austrian composer Arnold Schönberg in particular, whose atonal compositions result in what Adorno describes as "the renunciation of the customary crutches of a listening which always knows what to expect".¹⁰ In contrast to the formulaic, familiar structure of both popular and "classical" forms of music, Adorno argues that what is important about the discordant form of Schönberg's work is the degree to which it "fails to provide [the listener with] a safe centre for enjoyment".¹¹ Unlike "easy listening" music, which can be experienced in an absentminded, disengaged state, Adorno claims that the open, fragmentary structure of Schönberg's work prompts the listener to actively participate in the composition process. His music, he writes, "demands [...] not mere contemplation but praxis".¹²

In *Composing for the Films* (which Adorno co-wrote with Hanns Eisler in 1947) the role that a discordant music practice could play in actively stimulating audience participation is discussed in some depth. In a statement that echoes Adorno's criticism of the for-

---

9 | See also Schlingensief's reflections on this distinction in Christoph Schlingensief, *Ich weiß, ich war's*, ed. Aino Laberenz, Köln: Kiepenheuer & Witsch, 2012, p. 252.
10 | Adorno, Theodor W., "Arnold Schoenberg 1874-951" in: Theodor W. Adorno, *Prisms*, Cambridge, Mass.: The MIT Press, 1990, p. 149.
11 | Adorno, Theodor W., "The Dialectical Composer" in: *Essays on Music*, p. 203.
12 | Theodor W. Adorno, "Arnold Schoenberg 1874-1951", p. 150. Interestingly, Kluge has stated of the experimental form of his work that "[t]he basis is the Viennese School. What they said about music I believe is true for thought and poetry and novels and filmmaking". Stuart Liebman "On New German Cinema, Art, Enlightenment, and the Public Sphere: An Interview with Alexander Kluge", *October*, 46 (Fall, 1988), p. 58.

mulaic structure of popular music, Adorno and Eisler argue that "[o]ne of the most widespread prejudices in the motion-picture industry is the premise that the spectator should not be conscious of the music".[13] Instead of reinforcing what is taking place on screen, they argue that music should "throw its meaning into relief"[14] and, in the process, encourage the spectator to actively participate in the meaning-making process that is initiated, but not foreclosed, by the film in question. By generating a sense of discord between the music and the image on screen, the audience is not only made conscious of the music, but "[s]ound is robbed of its static quality and made dynamic by the ever-present factor of the 'unresolved'".[15]

Interestingly, this emphasis on an open, discordant, unresolved musical structure is also present in Schlingensief's reflections on the experimental form of his own work, which he compares to a musical composition that generates tension because its direction and meaning cannot easily be anticipated.[16] As revealed in the epigraph, Schlingensief rejects the "easily fabricated harmony" that Kluge associates with the reality principle. "The world", he states, "is asynchronous and I am atonal. [...] I have always worked atonally",[17] while in his analysis of *Kunst und Gemüse, A. Hipler* (*Art and Vegetables,*

---

**13** | Adorno, Theodor and Hanns Eisler, *Composing for the Films*, London and Atlantic Highlands: The Athlone Press, 1994, p. 9.
**14** | Ibid., p. 26.
**15** | Ibid., p. 41.
**16** | See, for example, Schlingensief's comments in this regard in Alexander Kluge, "Das Halten von Totenschädeln liegt mir nicht!/Christoph Schlingensief inszeniert Hamlet", p. 128. See also Alexander Kluge's delineation of Schlingensief's work as "musical theatre" in: Alexander Kluge, "Foreword" in *Christoph Schlingensief: Art Without Borders*, ed. Tara Forrest and Anna Teresa Scheer, Bristol and Chicago: Intellect, 2010, p. 3. "The way in which music moves", Kluge writes, "constitutes the essential form of [Schlingensief's] dramaturgy".
**17** | Christoph Schlingensief, "My work always has something to do with a change of perspective" (interviewed by Hans Ulrich Obrist) in: *AC: Christoph*

A. *Hipler*), a production he staged at the Volksbühne in 2004, Schlingensief goes a step further, stating that Schönberg's music provided him with an important "point of departure" and that his aim for the production was to develop a theatrical "counterpart" to Schönberg's work.[18] "On the stage", he writes, there is a "second music" that "one can see but cannot hear".[19]

While Schlingensief's observation that he has "always worked atonally" could be discussed in relation to his work in different fields, building on this idea of an atonal visual aesthetic, the specific aim of this chapter is to analyse the degree to which the discordant form of Schlingensief's 2002 television series *Freakstars 3000* cultivates the kind of active, creative mode of engagement that he associates with the production and experience of a non-reified form of pleasure.[20] Focusing on the 2003 film documentation of the program (also entitled *Freakstars 3000*), this chapter will explore how and with what effects Schlingensief has sought to cultivate an active, reflective mode of engagement by working firmly within – rather than outside – the mass-produced, standardised products of the culture industry. In doing so, I will argue that Schlingensief's work (discussed here and in the following chapter) undermines Adorno's insistent claim that

---

*Schlingensief – Church of Fear*, A. Koegel and K. König ed., Köln: Museum Ludwig and Verlag der Buchhandlung Walther König, 2005, p. 19.

**18 |** Christoph Schlingensief, *"Kunst und Gemüse: Eine Erklärung"* in: Christoph Schlingensief and Carl Hegemann, *Theater als Krankheit*, Berlin: Alexander Verlag, 2004, p. 2.

**19 |** Ibid.

**20 |** For Diedrich Diederichsen's analysis of Schlingensief's "dissonant" aesthetic, see "Diskursverknappungsbekämpfung und negatives Gesamtkunstwerk: Christoph Schlingensief und seine Musik" in: *Der Gesamtkünstler Christoph Schlingensief*, Pia Janke and Teresa Kovacs ed., Wien: Praesens, 2011, pp. 60-68.

"formulaic production eradicates critical or oppositional elements in culture".[21]

## Freakstars 3000

Since 1997, Schlingensief has produced five television series, three of which are organised around a variety talkshow format.[22] One of the standouts of the group, *Freakstars 3000*, was also modelled on a highly popular, mass-produced format: in this case, the casting show model popularised by programs such as *Popstars* and *Deutschland sucht den Superstar* (Germany seeks a Superstar). Although the structure, rules, and organization of the program are modelled closely on the casting show format, *Freakstars 3000* differs from other programs in the genre in the sense that it was shot at the Thiele Winkler Home for people with physical and mental disabilities in Lichtenrade, Berlin. The environs are thus less glamorous than the professional stages and rehearsal spaces in which programs such as *Popstars* take place and the contestants who perform for the panel (consisting of Schlingensief and two other judges) differ from the predominantly young, highly commodified types who ordinarily feature on such programs.

---

**21** | The phrase is from Deborah Cook, *The Culture Industry Revisited: Theodor W. Adorno on Mass* Culture, Lanham and London: Rowman & Littlefield, 1996, p. 109.

**22** | These include *Talk 2000* (1997), *U 3000* (2000), *Quiz 3000: Du Bist die Katastrophe* (*Quiz 3000: You are the Catastrophe*) (2002) and *Die Piloten* (The Pilots) (2007). Although the latter two series were not broadcast on television, Cordula Kablitz-Post has produced a film that documents the production of the *Die Piloten*. The documentary, also entitled *Die Piloten*, is available on DVD via Avanti Media, which has also released a DVD compilation of the *Talk 2000* episodes.

*Figure 1: Freakstars 3000.* © *Thomas Aurin*

In other regards, however, *Freakstars 3000* (which originally aired on the youth oriented popular music channel VIVA) reenacts the conventions of the format and charts the experiences and performances of the contestants as they participate in an audition and casting process that includes, among other activities: dance and vocal coaching workshops (the latter of which are conducted by Irm Hermann[23]); studio recording sessions; the formation of the band "*Mutter sucht Schrauben*" (Mother seeks Screws); the release of a CD[24]; and a "free jazz" concert at the Volksbühne in Berlin.

---

**23** | Irm Hermann is a German actress who appears frequently in Schlingensief's productions and was also a regular in the films of Rainer Werner Fassbinder.

**24** | *Schlingensiefs Freakstars 3000*, der hörverlag (2002).

*Figure 2: Freakstars 3000.* © *Thomas Aurin*

In keeping with the conventions of the format, we are also presented with behind-the-scenes footage of the contestants: Andreas, for example, takes us on a tour through his room that reveals AC/DC to be the source of his musical inspiration; Horst explains the work he previously undertook at a packing plant placing drills into boxes; Helga reveals that she cooks for her male housemates because "men are clumsy"; Eberhard plays air guitar and shares images from his family album with the audience; and Achim demonstrates how a bath lift functions to lower disabled residents into the water. The program was also supplemented by a web page that included contestant profiles and details about the hobbies and passions of the successful band members. Viewers were also encouraged to vote online for their favourite contestants, while a guestbook provided visitors with the opportunity to reflect on their thoughts about the show.[25]

---

**25** | See www.freakstars3000.de/. Last viewed February 8, 2015.

## Atonal Reenactment

Throughout his career, Schlingensief has frequently deployed a critical strategy of re-enactment in an attempt to facilitate public discussion and debate about a broad range of topics and issues. As discussed in the previous chapter, this strategy was most famously deployed in *Bitte Liebt Österreich* (2000) in which he staged a version of the *Big Brother* reality television series in an attempt to facilitate thinking, discussion and debate about the xenophobic, anti-immigration policies of Jörg Haider and the Freedom Party of Austria (FPÖ).[26] As I will explore in the following chapter, in 2002 Schlingensief also staged *Quiz 3000: Du bist die Katastrophe! (Quiz 3000: You are the Catastrophe!)* – a production that was modelled on the highly successful game show *Who wants to be a millionaire?*[27] As I will discuss in more detail, what is interesting about the production in the context of Schlingensief's "atonal" practice is the degree to which the questions posed to the contestants produce a jarring, discordant effect, in part because they deal with themes and issues pertaining to subjects that are largely avoided by the German entertainment media.

The integral relationship between Schlingensief's critical reenactment of popular, mass-produced, television formats and the

---

26 | See also Solveig Gade's analysis of the strategy of "performative recitation" employed by Schlingensief in the context of his 1998/1999 *Wahlkampfzircus – Chance 2000* (Election Circus – Chance 2000) in Solveig Gade, "Playing the Media Keyboard: The Political Potential of Performativity in Christoph Schlingensief's Electioneering Circus" in: Rune Gade and Anne Jerslev ed., *Performative Realism: Interdisciplinary Studies in Art and Media*, Copenhagen: Museum Tusculanum Press, 2005, pp. 19-49.

27 | For an overview of the performance, see Peter Kümmel, "Der Mann mit der Moralkelle. 'Ordnen Sie folgende KZ von Nord nach Süd': Christoph Schlingensief parodiert Günther Jauchs Rateshow", *Die Zeit*, No. 13 (21 March, 2002): http://www.zeit.de/2002/13/200213_quiz3000_xml. Last viewed 8 February, 2015.

self-described "atonal" character of his work is also rendered apparent in an interview with Alexander Kluge in which Schlingensief reflects on his "compulsion" to replay certain scenarios, characters, and events.[28] As he makes clear, however, this process of reenactment is not driven by a desire to generate an exact copy of that which is being reproduced. "If", he states, "I say, out of a desire for perfection, I can reenact it exactly, that's not it".[29] Rather, in a similar vein to Adorno's analysis of the sense of discord produced by atonal music, what fascinates Schlingensief about this mode of reenactment is the "inconsistency" that emerges as a result.[30]

In the opening scenes of *Freakstars 3000*, this "inconsistency" is immediately felt. The reproduction, however, is not a parody of the original because *Freakstars* sticks too closely to the conventions of the format, which are reinforced and undermined simultaneously. This dual process comes into play in the opening moments of the film via the male voiceover that introduces us – in a very familiar, generic tone – to what is to come: "Watch cool, young people, fulfil their dreams of a career in music, with talent and 100% percent dedication! Hear German originals use song to highlight the prob-

---

**28** | Schlingensief in Alexander Kluge, "Das Halten von Totenschädeln liegt mir nicht!/Christoph Schlingensief inszeniert Hamlet", p. 114.
**29** | Ibid., p. 128.
**30** | Jörg van der Horst has described this process as a form of "overdrawing": "Understanding by playing things through", he writes, "also means overpainting existing images and ideas. Originals were distorted but remained beneath the overdrawing as correctives". "In his television works", he continues, "Schlingensief applied playing through and painting over in rotation. He thus distorted existing images, while at the same time – through the distortion – making them discernible again, at least in broad strokes.". See Jörg van der Horst, "'So what was the actual truth? How did it all fit together?': Schlingensief, the Media and the Schlingensief Media" in: *Christoph Schlingensief*, ed. Klaus Biesenbach, Anna-Catharina Gebbers, Aino Laberenz, Susanne Pfeffer, London: Koenig Books, 2013, p. 140.

lems of the non-handicapped!"[31] This opening sequence is followed soon after by a Monty Pythonesque opening credit sequence that features, among other images, animated diagrams of a cross-section of a human brain and an anatomical measuring device that appears throughout the audition process. This montage sequence is followed by an image of one of the contestants, Horst Gelonneck, who stands at the front of the star-spangled stage and enthusiastically welcomes the audience to the show.

In the following scenes, which are located in the Thiele Winkler Home, Schlingensief stands before the contestants and explains how the audition process will proceed, while the voiceover states, in a very cheesy tone: "From Germany, Austria, and Switzerland, they've come from all over to fulfil their dream of becoming a real Freakstar 3000!" The following footage depicts the hopeful contestants as they receive their name tags, chat with Schlingensief and excitedly prepare for the audition. The build-up is too much for one of the contestants who shouts out in an aggressive tone, prompting another contestant – Bernhard – to leave the room in indignation. "Everyone is on edge", the voiceover states. "Tensions are running high. Jury member Christoph tries to calm them down".

Before the audition process begins, however, we are presented with a montage of clips which feature reproductions of a diverse range of television formats including, among others: *The Hit Parade*; a home shopping show; a weather program hosted by Schlingensief regular Mario Garzaner; and political talkshows entitled *Freakmann* (Freak Man) and *Presse Club* (Press Club) in which the politics of Jörg Haider, Hitler and the NPD (National Democratic Party) are discussed alongside other topics such as the status of the German press, and love and sex in contemporary Germany. Clips from each of these "programs" appear throughout the course of the

---

**31** | All quotes from the film are taken from the English language subtitles that appear on the *Freakstars 3000* DVD released by Filmgalerie 451 in 2003.

film, prompting viewers to consider the various ways in which other television formats could be reenacted and transformed as a result.[32]

Schlingensief's main focus, however, is the casting show format and, as the auditions begin, the gap between *Freakstars 3000* and its reality template immediately generates a sense of discord that produces a very interesting, destabilising effect. As Adorno and Eisler write in *Composing for the Films* of the discord generated by an experimental film scoring practice:

> [T]he aim of [...] an antithetic utilization of music will not be to introduce the largest possible number of dissonant sounds and novel colours into the machinery, which only spits them out again in a digested, blunted, and conventionalized form, but to break the mechanism of neutralization itself.[33]

In *Freakstars 3000*, the "dissolution of tonality"[34] produced by the "lack of fit" between the *Freakstars* contestants and the so-called "ideal" types who ordinarily feature on such programs immediately "break[s] the mechanism of neutralization" bestowed on such formats by a culture industry that thrives on the promotion of stereotypes and the reproduction of the status quo. Instead of a crowd full of Justin Timberlake or Beyoncé wannabes, we are presented with contestants of diverse ages and backgrounds who perform (some confidently, others tentatively) an eclectic collection of numbers, including: German folk tunes, an anti-war song by Udo Lindenberg, a selection of poems, and a song by Karel Gott, who was Austria's representative in the 1968 *Eurovision Song Contest*.

---

**32** | For a more detailed analysis of these clips and their relationship to the German programs on which they are based, see Morgen Koerner, "Subversions of the Medical Gaze: Disability and Media Parody in Christoph Schlingensiefs *Freakstars 3000*" in: *Cinema and Social Change in Germany and Austria*, ed. Gabriele Mueller, James M. Skidmore, Waterloo: Wilfrid Laurier University Press, 2012, pp. 66-68.
**33** | Theodor Adorno and Hanns Eisler, *Composing for the Films*, p. 87.
**34** | Ibid., p. 41, footnote 2.

The audition process kicks off with a performance by Ursel Plutowski – a self-described pensioner who "help[s] out with the washing". Immediately following her introduction, the image cuts to a picture of a human brain which descends on an animated chain from the top of the screen bearing the title "Nr. 1". The image then cuts back to Plutowski and, as she begins her performance, the aforementioned measuring device appears next to her head with her name superimposed across it. We see Schlingensief smile in support of her performance as he and the other jury members take notes at a desk while another contestant dances in the background. "Strong performance", the voiceover states. "Here comes contestant number two". The image of a brain bearing "Nr. 2" descends from the top of the screen and we cut to footage of Gisela's "grandiose performance". Later we hear from Kerstin ("a wonderful song, from a wonderful woman, who we won't be forgetting anytime soon") and Axel who performs a gentle version of "Wozu sind Kriege Da?" ("Why are there Wars?"). "Why are there wars?" the voiceover asks. "An important question nowadays. How will the jury react?" The image cuts to Schlingensief taking notes as he states: "No idea. Perhaps we should discuss that?" – a proposition enthusiastically embraced by one of the contestants who jumps up furiously and shouts "Yes, yes, yes, yes, yes!".

In contrast to the judgemental atmosphere which pervades the casting show format, the mood generated by the audition process is predominantly light-hearted and positive and Schlingensief is very supportive in encouraging those participants who are nervous and/or lacking in confidence. When Werner Brecht, for example, declares that he only received a C minus in music, Schlingensief states that he himself received an F, and Brecht's audition proceeds with the support of Sabrina, another contestant. "An example", the voiceover states, "of unbridled solidarity between our candidates. The jury is impressed". When Horst, who was initially lacking in confidence, manages to produce a tune, Schlingensief reflects: "It was great how you just sang Horst; even though you said you can't. Sometimes you are better than you think. It was great. Thanks. Applause". Later, the jury ensures that contestants who don't make it into the subsequent rounds are left confident of their abilities. As Schlingensief explains to Andreas, the AC/DC fan who plays the guitar: "You like AC/DC but our band probably only plays free jazz. So the stuff you do, the AC/DC, wouldn't fit with the band".

More generally, the "lack of fit" between *Freakstars 3000* and the casting show format generates much humour not because, as some critics have suggested, Schlingensief is "making fun" of the disabled contestants, but because the program is highly effective in rendering viewers conscious of the stereotypes, norms, and clichés according to which the casting show (and other formats) operate.[35] When Mario, for example, reenacts a weather show by slapping cardboard cut-outs of clouds and sun motifs on a flimsy background that keeps falling down, attention is drawn to the highly staged, constructed "nature" of such programs with their glamorous presenters and high-tech graphics. Indeed *Freakstars 3000* is very successful in undermining the neutral, automated mode of engagement that Adorno associates with the standardised products of the culture industry, because it encourages the audience to question how – and with what effects – such products actively shape our perception of what it means to be "normal" or "disabled". As the cheesy voiceover informs us in the opening minutes of the film, song is employed in *Freakstars 3000* "to highlight the problems of the non-handicapped", and it is clearly the perceived prejudices and shortcomings of the audience –

---

**35** | For Schlingensief's analysis of his desire to render popular "prototypes" and "mechanisms" "recognisable", see his reflections on *Chance 2000* in Schlingensief, *Ich weiß, ich war's*, p. 59. As Solveig Gade argues in her analysis of *Chance 2000:* "In his performative recitation of the discourses of media society, a number of recitations happen, offering a difference in the form of a change of perspective. A change of perspective concerning the discourses produced by media society. Discourses that gradually have been encoded so efficiently into the consciousness of the citizens that they are no more reflected critically or consciously upon". Gade, "Playing the Media Keyboard", p. 42.

rather than any "shortcomings" of the contestants themselves – at which Schlingensief's criticism is levelled.[36]

In Schlingensief's productions, however, criticism is never straightforward. Indeed, as attested by the open, ambiguous form characteristic of his work, he is not driven by a desire to pedagogically instruct the audience on the "best way" to approach the issues and ideas raised by his productions.[37] Rather, in keeping with his delineation of a non-alienated form of pleasure, his work encourages the audience to reflect on their own prejudices and to think critically and creatively about the material at hand. Schlingensief himself describes this active, critical mode of engagement as a form of "self-

---

**36** | As Rudi Zander reflects in a backstage interview that appears towards the end of the film: "Through the medium of televised broadcast, I would say that a broad audience will consider the problems of the non-handicapped and thereby receive stimulus to do similar or different things". The image then cuts to footage of the band at their debut performance as Kerstin sings: "Miracles happen again and again. Today or tomorrow. They will happen". See also Jörg van der Horst's analysis of the degree to which the program encouraged viewers to rethink the concept of disability. "The 'freak stars'", he writes, "the crazies by consensus, quite candidly asked the Main Street member of the television audience who and what was actually handicapped here: the residents of the home? – or rather the mechanical people in the closed television institutions – the alpenglowing folk musicians in their ideal-world hoedown, the noisy propagandists of the home-shopping channels, the ethical-synthetic parade celebrities prizing the asceptic, damp-mopped Germany in state-funded commercials, or the press clubs, the journalistic elite who chatter every trouble spot on earth into the ground by all the rules in the instruction manual ...?". Jörg van der Horst, '"So what was the actual truth? How did it all fit together?'": Schlingensief, the Media and the Schlingensief Media", in *Christoph Schlingensief*, p. 141.

**37** | See, for example, Schlingensief's comments in this regard in relation to a discussion about *Bitte Liebt* Österreich, in Alexander Kluge, "Theater der Handgreiflichkeit/Christoph Schlingensief's Wiener Container", *News & Stories*, SAT 1 (October 22, 2000).

provocation" because he argues that it is the responsibility of the viewer to work through the feelings, issues, and prejudices aroused in them by the material in question.[38] In a similar vein to Adorno's delineation of the active, creative mode of engagement fostered by Schönberg's atonal compositions, Schlingensief's atonal reenactment of the casting show format challenges the audience to become active co-producers in the meaning-making process.

## Tell me what to think

As revealed by the large number of viewer comments entered on the *Freakstars 3000* online guestbook[39], not all members of the audience are comfortable with Schlingensief's provocative, non-pedagogical approach. In keeping with Adorno's analysis of the passive, non-participatory mode of reception fostered by the culture industry, a number of viewers noted that they felt uncomfortable while watching the film because they were unsure how they were *supposed* to respond.[40] "I want to know", one viewer noted,

---

**38** | Schlingensief quoted in Anonymous, "Keine Wiener-'Konzentrationswoche'", *Die Presse*, June 7 (2000).
**39** | The guestbook can be found at: http://www.freakstars3000.de/. Last accessed 15 April, 2009.
**40** | As Deborah Cook argues in her analysis of Adorno's writings on popular culture: "The main effect that schemata have on viewers is to condition or encourage them to understand their own experiences unreflectively in a way similar to that found in the media". She argues that "[t]his effect is bolstered by the pseudo-realism of cultural commodities; the schemata or patterns found in television and film have an even greater impact on viewers because these media reproduce everyday life in such 'realistic' detail." See Deborah Cook, *The Culture Industry Revisited: Theodor W. Adorno on Mass* Culture, Lanham and London: Rowman & Littlefield, 1996, p. 46. In this context, Schlingensief's employment of the casting show template to generate ambiguity rather than confirm the status quo was, as the following

whether I can die laughing without thinking about my morals or whether what has been concocted there is serious? [...] I find it simply so priceless. [...] Am, however, really SERIOUSLY confused. Have unfortunately absolutely NO idea what it is.[41]

"The three of us", another viewer wrote,

are watching the film and we don't know what is meant by it. Should we be reflective, amused, or disgusted? [...] We have come to the conclusion that the whole production is a send-up of disabled people and that such a thing should not, under any circumstances, be broadcast on television.[42]

The comments of another viewer expressed a similar sentiment:

Am I just humourless, full of prejudice, not prepared to see sick and disabled people on television? No idea. [...] In any case, I was thinking about how remarkably far our (German?) society has developed since the Third Reich and Hitler: then, all "freaks" were locked away or "euthenised", we have now come so far that we amuse ourselves at their cost, and thoroughly take the Mickey out of them, in order to then celebrate what liberal and unprejudiced people we are![43]

The view expressed both here and in the previous quote, that Schlingensief is simply making fun of the disabled contestants, is one that was well represented in both the media and in guestbook comments that appeared at the time of the film's release. However, in their

---

quotes from the guestbook demonstrate, both confusing and unnerving for some viewers.
**41** | *Freakstars 3000 Gästebuch*, entry 27 (August 10, 2004). Last accessed 15 April, 2009.
**42** | *Freakstars 3000 Gästebuch*, entry 20 (August 10, 2004). Last accessed 15 April, 2009.
**43** | *Freakstars 3000 Gästebuch*, entry 51 (August 10, 2004). Last accessed 15 April, 2009.

ambivalence about the appropriateness of featuring disabled people on such a program, such comments would seem to support, rather than undermine one of the key points that Schlingensief is seeking to make: That "[t]he freak is the situation itself, which forces us to make a distinction between what is and isn't normal".[44]

As Schlingensief makes clear, the discomfort experienced by some viewers while watching the film/program could be seen as a hangover from the Third Reich and from Nazi policies according to which the contestants would, indeed, be viewed as "freaks". These policies, which were put in place in the 1930s, dictated – among other things – that the "hereditarily defective" be sterilized and/or "euthenised" in order to "cleanse" the German *Volk*.[45] Schlingensief is very upfront in seeking to make this connection explicit. By introducing anatomical measuring devices at the start of the program, and by superimposing images of those devices on footage of contestants as they participate in the audition process, Schlingensief confronts viewers to question the degree to which certain National Socialist ideals of what constitutes a "normal", "healthy", and/or "desirable" citizen retain a certain currency in the contemporary media and popular culture spheres.[46]

---

**44** | Schlingensief, quoted in Johanna Straub, "Wir sind alle krank", *Spiegel Online* (November 19, 2003): http://www.spiegel.de/kultur/kino/0,1518, 274587,00.html Last accessed 8 February, 2009.

**45** | Carol Poore *Disability in Twentieth Century German Culture*, Ann Arbor: University of Michigan Press, 2007, pp. 75-78. This book provides a comprehensive analysis of the representation of disability in German culture spanning the Weimar period up until the early years of the twenty-first century.

**46** | Schlingensief has also reflected on this in response to public criticism of the fact that he discussed his illness in the media: "Should we all", he writes, "dutifully remain silent in order not to disturb these screaming images of health on TV? Supermodels, strong hair, white teeth, Adonis bodies [...] and us sick people are too loud?" Christoph Schlingensief, *Ich weiß, ich war's*, p. 10.

As is the case with much of Schlingensief's work, this questioning is prompted by a process of reenactment: in this case via the playing out – and evocation of – names and policies that are clearly derogatory and that, during the Third Reich, resulted in mass murder. In this context, the title *Freakstars 3000* serves as a provocation to (rather than an expression of solidarity with) those audience members who view the public representation of disabled people as somehow "inappropriate", "distasteful", or "uncomfortable". Through the presentation of interviews in which the contestants discuss their lives, loves and interests, and by providing a very diverse group of people with a space in which they can express their enthusiasm for singing, dance, free jazz, collaboration and performance, Schlingensief challenges the audience to question why – and with what effects – disabled people are largely excluded from the public image of reality generated by the media.[47]

---

**47** | The fact that the *Freakstars* band, Mutter sucht Schrauben, primarily produces free jazz is interesting in the context of Adorno's trenchant critique of what he describes as the highly "standardized", "formulaic" structure of commercial jazz. As Ulrich Schönherr, however, has pointed out: "Despite Adorno's harsh criticism, one can still find in his jazz studies passages which describe, at least *ex negativo*, utopian elements in jazz: 'If one had drawn the consequences out of the syncopation and the rhythmic-improvisatory impulses, then the old symmetry and therefore also the structure of tonal harmony would have collapsed ... then jazz would have lost its consumability and its easy intelligibility and would have changed into 'artistic' music. ... Jazz didn't engage in such ventures'". As Schönherr, however, makes clear: "The innovative practice of jazz since the late 1950s and the explosion-like radicalization of the music in the 1960s by musicians such as Ornette Coleman, John Coltrane, Charles Mingus and Anthony Braxton has largely fulfilled what Adorno had not seen realized in jazz". Ulrich Schönherr, "Adorno and Jazz: Reflections on a Failed Encounter", *Telos*, Number 87 (Spring, 1991), p. 93. For Adorno's critique of the "formulaic" structure of commercial jazz, see Theodor W. Adorno, "Perennial Fashion" in: Theodor W. Adorno, *Prisms*, Cambridge, Mass: The MIT Press, 1990.

*Figure 3: Freakstars 3000.* © *Thomas Aurin*

In stark contrast to Adorno's delineation of standardised television formats that "channelize audience reaction" and promote an "identification with the status quo"[48], the significance of *Freakstars 3000* lies in the degree to which it encourages viewers – in a playful, humorous, but nonetheless serious way – to think critically and creatively for themselves. Moreover, by reproducing the form and effects of an experimental, atonal music practice within the structure of a popular and widely accessible television format, Schlingensief has gone some way to bridging the gap between art and popular culture: those "torn halves of an integral freedom" which, for Adorno, "[did] not add up".[49]

---

**48** | Theodor W. Adorno, "How to Look at Television" in: *The Culture Industry: Selected Essays on Mass Culture*, ed. J.M. Bernstein, London and New York: Routledge, 2001, pp.165 and 164.

**49** | See Adorno's letter to Walter Benjamin (dated March 18, 1936) in: Ernst Bloch, Georg Lukacs, Bertolt Brecht, Walter Benjamin, Theodor Adorno, *Aesthetics and Politics*, London and New York: Verso, 1990, p. 123.

# CHAPTER 5

From Information to Experience:

Schlingensief's *Quiz 3000*

> The curiosity which transforms the world into objects is not objective: it is not concerned with what is known but with the fact of knowing it, with having, with knowledge as a possession. This is precisely how the objects of information are organized today. [...] As facts they are arranged in such a way that they can be grasped as quickly and easily as possible. Wrenched from all context, detached from thought, they are made instantly accessible to an infantile grasp.
>
> THEODOR W. ADORNO[1]

> It is about the desire to feel something in a world that kills *Erlebnis*.
>
> CHRISTOPH SCHLINGENSIEF[2]

---

**1** | Theodor W. Adorno, "The Schema of Mass Culture" in: Theodor W. Adorno, *The Culture* Industry: *Selected Essays on Mass Culture*, ed. J.M. Bernstein, London and New York: Routledge, 2001, p. 85.

**2** | Christoph Schlingensief, "Betroffenheitstypen" in: Christoph Schlingensief and Carl Hegemann, *Chance 2000: Wähle Dich selbst*, Köln: Kiepenheuer &Witsch, 1998, p. 17.

In a pilot episode of his third talkshow *Die Piloten* (The Pilots) that was shot at the Akademie der Künste in 2007, Christoph Schlingensief participates in a heated debate with two of his guests about the mode of engagement facilitated by the exhibits at the former concentration camp in Dachau.³ Reflecting on his visit there as a sixteen year old school student, Schlingensief describes the displays that prompt one to "look at this" and "look at that" as "reconstructions" that "mount something that I should feel [*empfinden*] but which I can't really feel at all". Responding to his guest's defence of the camp as an "information centre", Schlingensief's frustrated retort provides us with an insight into what he thinks the site should be: "Not an information centre, but an experience centre [*Erfahrungszentrum*]!"⁴

The distinction that Schlingensief draws in this statement – between information and experience – is central to Walter Benjamin's analysis of the decline in the capacity for experience (*Erfahrung*) that he associates with the rise of an information-driven news culture. Taking newspapers as his prime example, Benjamin argues that "[i]f it were the intention of the press to have the reader assimilate the information it supplies as part of his experience, it would not achieve its purpose". "But its intention", he claims, "is just the opposite and it is achieved: to isolate events from the realm in which they could affect the experience of the reader".⁵ This segregation process is accomplished by the fragmented format of newspapers and by the

---

3 | The guests include Lea Rosh (a journalist and key figure behind the establishment of the Memorial to the Murdered Jews in Berlin) and German Greens politician Claudia Roth.

4 | Cordula Kablitz-Post (director), *Christoph Schlingensief: Die Piloten* (2009).

5 | Kluge, too, argues that the mainstream media has "little patience for the substance of experience". Alexander Kluge, "It is a mistake to think that the dead are dead" in: *The Power of Intellectuals in Contemporary Germany*, ed. Michael Geyer, Chicago and London: University of Chicago Press, 2001, p. 215.

emphasis on "brevity", "newness", and immediate comprehension characteristic of the individual news bites; qualities that impact negatively on the reader's capacity to reflect on – and participate in the meaning-making process about – the issues, ideas, and events in question.[6]

Benjamin's comments on this nexus – between the proliferation of information as a mode of communication and the decline in the capacity for experience and autonomous thought – form part of a larger argument about the diminution in the quality of life that he associates with the replacement of *Erfahrung* by *Erlebnis*. As will become clear, these terms not only form the two poles of Benjamin's theory of experience; they are also central to Schlingensief's conception of the significant role the mass media plays in stunting, rather than enhancing the capacity to engage with issues and ideas in an autonomous, affective, and meaningful way.

In what follows, I will summarise Benjamin's bipartite theory of experience and draw out the connections between his concept of *Erlebnis* and Theodor Adorno's delineation of the passive, consumer-oriented mode of experience fostered by the information-driven format of the culture industry. The focus of this chapter is not, however, these ideas *per se* but rather, building on ideas explored in the previous chapter, I will analyse the important role that Schlingensief's television programs have played in undermining the indifferent, perfunctory mode of experience that Adorno associates with the mass media. Through an analysis of the pilot episode of Schlingensief's 2002 reality program *Quiz 3000: Du bist die Katastrophe!* (Quiz 3000: You are the Catastrophe!), this chapter will explore how – and with what effects – Schlingensief has sought to transform the information-driven focus of television quiz shows into a source of experience for viewers and contestants alike. Drawing on Kluge's delineation of the task of a realistic method, I will argue that *Quiz*

---

**6** | Walter Benjamin, "On Some Motifs in Baudelaire" in: *Selected Writings, Volume 4*, eds. Howard Eiland and Michael Jennings, Cambridge, Mass.: Harvard University Press, 2003, p. 315.

*3000* encourages the contestant/audience to reflect on German politics (both past and present) in a manner that is thoughtful, self-determined and engaged and, in doing so, asks them to interrogate (rather than passively consume) the limited, hegemonic image of reality propagated by the mainstream news media.

## ERFAHRUNG AND ERLEBNIS

In keeping with his delineation of the isolated, perfunctory mode of experience cultivated by information, Benjamin describes *Erlebnis* as a form of experience that one registers consciously, the content of which makes a superficial impression that is superseded by the following moment. This type of experience is lacking in substance because consciousness "assigns an incident a precise point in time in consciousness, at the cost of the integrity of the incident's contents" and, in doing so, transforms it "into an isolated experience [*Erlebnis*]."[7] In a letter to Adorno, both the superficial nature and sense of temporal deferral characteristic of this mode of experience are described by Benjamin in concrete terms. "There is", he writes,

no reason to make a secret of the fact that I trace the roots of "my theory of experience [*Erfahrung*]" to a childhood memory. My parents naturally took walks with us wherever we spent our summers. There were either two or three of us children. The one I have in mind is my brother. After we had visited one of the obligatory tourist attractions around Freudenstadt, Wengen, or Schreiberhau, my brother used to say, "Now we can say that we've been there." This statement made an unforgettable impression on me.[8]

---

7 | Ibid., p. 319.

8 | Gershom Scholem and Theodor W. Adorno ed., *The* Correspondence *of Walter Benjamin: 1910*-1940, Chicago and London: The University of Chicago Press, 1994, p. 629. Theodor W. Adorno and Walter Benjamin, *Briefwechsel: 1928-1940*, ed. Henri Lonitz, Frankfurt am Main: Suhrkamp, 1994, p. 424.

Benjamin's brother's statement is a very apt description of the detached, impassive mode of experience that Benjamin describes as *Erlebnis*. The sites in question do not, presumably, leave a lasting impression on the young tourist. Rather experience, in this context, is transformed into something reminiscent of a snapshot or souvenir; a possession or object that does little more than attest to the fact that he has "been there".[9]

This conception of experience as something that one *has* or *consumes* shares a number of similarities with Adorno's delineation of the consumer-oriented mode of engagement fostered by the information-driven focus of the mass media. As his comments in the epigraph make clear, for Adorno, information refers to "facts" and ideas that are easily consumed because they are "pre-digested".[10] In keeping with Benjamin's analysis of information as that which can be immediately understood, the "pre-digested" facts described by Adorno support, rather than challenge the status quo. "Information", he writes, "refers constantly to what has been preformed, to what others already know. To be informed about something implies an enforced solidarity with what has already been judged".[11]

Adorno's criticism of information forms part of a larger argument about the decline in productivity and experience fostered by

---

**9** | In "Central Park" Benjamin describes the souvenir as "the complement to isolated experience [*das Kompliment des 'Erlebnisses'*]. In it is precipitated the increasing self-estrangement of human beings whose past is inventoried with dead effects". See Benjamin, *Selected Writings, Vol. 4*, ed. Howard Eiland and Michael W. Jennings, Cambridge, Mass. and London, England, p. 183 and "Zentralpark" in: Walter Benjamin, *Gesammelte Schriften*, ed. Rolf Tiedemann and Hermann Schweppenhäuser, vol. 1.2, Frankfurt am Main: Suhrkamp, 1974, p. 681.

**10** | See Adorno, "The Schema of Mass Culture", p. 67. He writes: "The pre-digested quality of the product prevails, justifies itself and establishes itself all the more firmly in so far as it constantly refers to those who cannot digest anything not already pre-digested. It is baby food".

**11** | Adorno, "The Schema of Mass Culture", p. 84.

the standardised products of the culture industry. As discussed in the previous chapter, underpinning his argument is an acknowledgement of the damage wrought by alienated labour conditions that leave people feeling exhausted, bored, and unfulfilled. Benjamin too points to production-line labour to illustrate the decline in the capacity to draw on one's experience which, for him, is symptomatic of *Erlebnis*. In contrast to the emphasis on practice which is central to the art of craftsmanship, in which the capacity to draw on one's experience is vital to the development of one's practice, Benjamin argues that the "drilling of the workers" in production-line labour makes "a speciality out of the absence of all development". "The unskilled worker", he writes, "is the one most deeply degraded by the drill of the machines. His work has been sealed off from experience [*Erfahrung*]"[12]

This description – of the temporal isolation and experience of fragmentation characteristic of production-line labour – is also echoed in Adorno's analysis of the superficial, distracted mode of perception fostered by the mainstream media. "[N]o one", he writes, "is trusted to remember anything that has already happened or to concentrate upon anything other than what is presented to him in the given moment. The consumer is thus reduced to the abstract present'; someone who is "incapable of ... exercising thought."[13]

*Erfahrung*, on the other hand, overcomes the temporal fragmentation characteristic of *Erlebnis* because, for Benjamin, it designates a form of experience that amalgamates the past and the present. As he makes clear, this is because *Erfahrung* is informed by the past experiences of the subject in question. In contrast to *Erlebnis*, it is not characterised by easy comprehension, but by a form of reflection that is guided, in part, by the senses and that doesn't, as a result, always find itself on solid ground. "I have experience [*Erfahrung*]",

---

**12** | Benjamin, "On Some Motifs in Baudelaire", p. 133 and "Über einige Motive bei Baudelaire" in: Walter Benjamin, *Gesammelte Schriften*, vol. 1.2, p. 632.
**13** | Adorno, "The Schema of Mass Culture", p. 69.

Benjamin (quoting Franz Kafka) states, "'and I am not joking when I say that it is a seasickness on dry land.'"[14]

What is crucial here is that the experiential vertigo characteristic of *Erfahrung* initiates a feeling and thinking process in which the responsibility for generating meaning is relegated to the subject in question.[15] In contrast to *Erlebnis* which is given "a classificatory number behind which it disappears" ("'So now we've been there.' ('I've had an experience')"[16], *Erfahrung* oscillates between the past and the present and is mediated by a subject who forges his/her own autonomous connections between the two. If, as Adorno states, it is "productivity – the ability to bring forth something that was not already there" which has been "eradicated" by information[17], then *Erfahrung* is marked by a productive engagement with the material and ideas in question. In contrast to the emphasis on easy comprehension that Benjamin associates with *Erlebnis*, *Erfahrung* designates a form of production that Kluge describes as *"experience in the production of experience"* (*"Erfahrung in der Produktion von Erfahrung"*).[18]

---

**14** | Walter Benjamin, "Franz Kafka: On the Tenth Anniversary of His Death" in: Walter Benjamin, *Selected Writings, Volume 2*, ed. Michael W. Jennings, Howard Eiland and Gary Smith, Cambridge, Mass.: Harvard University Press, 1999. p. 809.
**15** | As Schlingensief makes clear, *Erfahrung* is about discovery, the desire to discover something anew. See Christoph Schlingensief, *Ich weiß, ich war's*, ed. Aino Laberenz, Köln: Kiepenheuer & Witsch, 2012, p. 20.
**16** | Walter Benjamin, *The Arcades Project*, ed. Rolf Tiedemann, Cambridge, Mass.: Harvard University Press, 1999, H5, 1, p. 211.
**17** | Theodor W. Adorno, "Free Time" in Adorno, *The Culture* Industry, p. 193.
**18** | Alexander Kluge, "The Sharpest Ideology: That Reality Appeals to its Realistic Character" in: *Alexander Kluge: Raw Materials For the Imagination*, ed. Tara Forrest, Amsterdam: Amsterdam University Press, 2012, p. 194 and Alexander Kluge "Die schärfste Ideologie: daß Realität sich auf ihre realistischen Charakter beruft" in: Alexander Kluge, *Gelegenheitsarbe-*

Returning to Schlingensief's comments about the former concentration camp in Dachau and his criticism of the information-oriented displays that direct one to "look at this" and "look at that", we can begin to get a sense of what he means when he states that the exhibits display material that he "should feel but which [he] can't really feel at all". Clearly, what is at issue here is not an inability, on Schlingensief's behalf, to recognise the atrocities that occurred there (he acknowledges, after all, that the material in question is something he "should feel"). Rather, what drives his criticism is a concern about the degree of desensitisation that occurs when the history of the camp – and the horrors that took place there – are packaged as information for public consumption. When Schlingensief advocates an "experience" rather than an "information" centre, he is calling for a site that encourages visitors to participate in the meaning-making process themselves; to draw productively on their own experience, and the experience of others; and to invest time, feeling, and energy in grappling with (rather than simply registering or consuming) the images, spaces, materials, and ideas with which they are presented.

## REALISM AS PROTEST

Schlingensief's criticism of information as a mode of communication is not specific to debates about the memorialisation of the Holocaust, but forms part of a larger argument about the shift from production to consumption precipitated by a media dominated, consumer-oriented culture that he describes as "System 1". In a similar vein to Adorno's analysis of the passive mode of engagement fostered by the culture industry, what troubles Schlingensief about this system is the degree to which it stifles independent thought and promotes an acceptance of the status quo. "System 2" – the title he employs to describe the modus operandi of his work – seeks to

---

*it einer Sklavin. Zur realistischen Methode*, Frankfurt am Main: Suhrkamp Verlag, 1975, p. 219.

undermine the emphasis on easy consumption promoted by System 1 and to foster, in the process, reflection, debate, and autonomous thought. As Schlingensief's comment in the epigraph makes clear, System 2 (and, by extension, his work more generally) is motivated by "the desire to feel something in a world that kills *Erlebnis*."[19]

As the reality productions he produced prior to *Quiz 3000* make clear, Schlingensief has experimented with different formats in an attempt to frustrate the emphasis on easy comprehension that Benjamin associates with *Erlebnis*.[20] For Benjamin, it is precisely by cultivating this superficial, perfunctory mode of engagement that the mainstream media functions to stymie debate about how – and with what effects – the so-called "reality" in which we live could be transformed into something very different. For both Schlingensief and Kluge, the image of reality generated by the media (and by politicians and the culture industry more generally) is a "simulation of reality"[21] that not only excludes the needs and interests of large sectors of the population, but which stunts the capacity to conceive of the degree to which things could, in fact, be very different. To reiterate a point made earlier, the so-called "real" state of affairs "is not necessarily or certainly real". Alternative possibilities "also belong to reality. The realistic result, the actual result is only an abstraction that has murdered all other possibilities for the moment".[22] Within this schema, a "realistic" approach that is true to its name is neither limited nor governed by the current state of affairs. On the contrary, to be "realistic" is to be mindful of the fact that the so-called "reality"

---

**19** | Schlingensief, "Betroffenheitstypen", p. 17.

**20** | As discussed in the previous chapters, these include *Bitte Liebt Österreich* and *Freakstars 3000*.

**21** | See Kluge's television program "Die Kirche der Angst/Erste attaistische Nachrichten von Christoph Schlingensief", *News & Stories*, SAT 1 (24 August, 2003).

**22** | Jan Dawson, '"But Why are the Questions so Abstract?': An Interview with Alexander Kluge" in Jan Dawson, *Alexander Kluge and the Occasional Work of a Female Slave*, New York: Zoetrope, 1977, p. 34.

in which we live is neither given nor set in stone, but rather open to change; a reality that can be transformed according to the will and desire of people who "actually [....] want something completely different".²³

Extrapolating on these ideas in relation to Schlingensief's television experiments, it is clear that if "reality" television is to live up to the promise inherent in its name, then its task is not to reflect or confirm the status quo, but to encourage viewers to think critically and imaginatively about the possibilities and limitations of the world in which they live. "The uncompromising production of realistic products is itself"', Kluge writes, "the means of changing the horizon of experience"'.²⁴ "The motive for realism is never the confirmation of reality but protest".²⁵ Within this schema, the success of a realistic text is judged according to the degree to which it engages the viewer at the level of his/her own experience. Building on Benjamin's delineation of *Erfahrung*, Kluge argues that the kind of experience in question is characterised by an imaginative, autonomous, and sensorially engaged mode of reflection that, above all, questions – rather than accepts – the status quo.

While the realistic method employed by Kluge in his experimental film and television productions is distinguished by an emphasis on fragmentation and an extensive use of mixed materials, Schlingensief's approach is very different in the sense that his reality programs operate within – rather than outside of – the standardised television formats he critiques. As I will argue in the following section via an analysis of *Quiz 3000*, it is by corrupting these formats that Schlingensief undermines the automated mode of engagement facilitated by the audience's familiarity with the programs in question, rendering it near impossible for viewers to consume the programs in a passive, unreflective way.

---

**23** | Alexander Kluge, "The Sharpest Ideology: That Reality Appeals to its Realistic Character", p. 191.
**24** | Ibid., p. 194.
**25** | Ibid., p. 192.

## *QUIZ 3000:* *YOU ARE THE CATASTROPHE*

> The concept of progress must be grounded in the idea of catastrophe. The fact that things are status quo *is* the catastrophe.[26]
> WALTER BENJAMIN

> However useful it might be from a practical point of view to have as much information as possible at one's disposal, there still prevails the iron law that the information in question shall never touch the essential, shall never degenerate into thought.[27]
> THEODOR W. ADORNO

The pilot episode of *Quiz 3000* was shot in 2002 at the Volksbühne in Berlin and subsequently toured as a stage production to theatres in Germany and Switzerland.[28] Modelled closely on the popular reality program *Who Wants to Be a Millionaire?* (the German version of which, hosted by Günther Jauch, has screened on RTL since 1999) *Quiz 3000* is, as I will explore in more detail, remarkable in the way it seeks to transform the information-driven focus of television quiz shows into a source of experience for viewers and contestants alike.

The pilot program opens with images of Schlingensief as host (wearing a lustrous grey suit and a spotty tie) striking a series of pos-

---

26 | Benjamin, "Central Park", *Selected Writings*, Vol. 4, pp. 184-5.
27 | Adorno, "The Schema of Mass Culture", p. 84.
28 | My analysis of the performance/program is based on the production that took place at the Volksbühne in Berlin on March 15 and 16, 2002. The production that toured to other theatres in Germany and Switzerland throughout 2002 changed over time and differed in a number of key regards from the original work. I am grateful to Frieder Schlaich for providing me with a copy of the Volksbühne production.

es to music as a montage of footage from a range of different news, talk, and current affairs programs flashes behind him on screen. Although the opening sequence is followed by the title "The prototype for a new quiz show", when Schlingensief enters and the set is revealed (featuring a round table, a pair of stools, and two back-to-back computer monitors on a podium) it is immediately apparent that *Quiz 3000* is a re-enactment of *Who Wants to be a Millionaire?*

Figure 1: *Quiz 3000*. © Thomas Aurin

*Millionaire*, like other programs in the genre, is organised around a question and answer format. Both the contestant and the host are seated at a table with a computer monitor on which to focus. The contestant, who is presented with multiple choice questions, is asked to "lock in" one of four possible answers that appear before them on screen. With each question that is answered correctly, the contestant moves up a ten-point scale that starts at 100 and ends with 1,000,000 Euros. If the contestant becomes stuck, they are provided with a series of "lifelines" or, in the case of *Quiz 3000*, "jokers". These jokers allow contestants to seek advice from the studio audience, a friend/family member, and/or one of several on-site "VIPs". The question and answer process is also accompanied by discussions initiated by the host, who asks the contestant about his/her life and interests and speculates (without giving too much away) on which of the four possible answers is correct. As I will discuss in more detail, in *Quiz 3000* Schlingensief also endeavours to situate the question in a broader political and/or historical context in an attempt to stimulate reflection, discussion, and debate about the issues and ideas at hand. If the contestant is able to answer all ten questions correctly, they are awarded the 1,000,000 prize.[29] If, however, the contestant "locks in" an incorrect answer, they are replaced by another contestant who begins the process again by starting at the bottom of the scale.

The questions that appear on *Millionaire?* largely conform to the "pre-digested" data that Adorno associates with information because they revolve around facts pertaining to fields such as geography, biology, history, sport, music, and popular culture that are generally agreed to be true. Questions such as "Who won seven gold medals at the 1972 Olympic Games?", "A popular form of American folk music is called Country & …?", and "Where in the human body does one find the cruciate ligament?"[30] are very straightforward and provide little cause, following Adorno's sarcastic formulation, for *Erlebnis* to "degenerate into thought". In a similar vein to the detached, impersonal mode of experience that Benjamin associates with his sightseeing brother, knowledge – in this context – functions as a commodity that one has or consumes. "We agree", Adorno states, "with the majority about it, yet simultaneously we wish to deprive them of it and take possession of it ourselves."[31]

For Adorno, the information-driven focus of quiz shows thus has two important functions. Firstly, it "socializes" the "curiosity"[32]

---

**29** | In *Quiz 3000*, this jackpot was downscaled to a briefcase of banknotes and a second-hand car.
**30** | These questions all featured on the German version of *Who Wants to Be a Millionaire?*
**31** | Adorno, "The Schema of Mass Culture", p. 84.
**32** | Ibid.

of those hungry for knowledge by providing them with "pre-digested" information bites that stunt – rather than promote – independent thought. Secondly, it provides a sense of solace to those for whom their own "experience proves inadequate". "[T]he apparatus", he writes, "trains [them] to appear well-informed on pain of losing prestige among other people and to renounce the more arduous process of real experience [umständlichen Erfahrung]." "[T]his", he adds "is where information leaps in: ... sparing each individual from the disgrace of appearing as stupid as everyone else."[33]

This mode of knowledge acquisition is, for Adorno, not specific to the quiz show format, but is a defining characteristic of the kind of communication fostered by the culture industry more generally. Schlingensief, too, argues in a similar vein that television, in particular, plays an important role in inculcating spectators into accepting the status quo. Playing on the connotations of the German word for watching television (*fernsehen* = far or distant seeing), Schlingensief concludes that "the person who does little more than watch television is also little more than a *Fernseher*"[34]: that is, someone who views the world from afar, who is a passive consumer, rather than an active participant in, or producer of the "reality" on screen.

Returning to *Quiz 3000* and to Kluge's conception of the task of a realistic method, it is clear that Schlingensief's realistic re-enactment of the quiz show format is not driven by a desire to produce an exact copy of *Millionaire*. Rather, as Schlingensief has made clear in the interview with Kluge cited in the previous chapter, what fascinates him about re-enactment as a critical strategy are the inconsistencies generated in the reproduction process that serve as catalysts

---

33 | Ibid., pp. 81–82 and "Das Schema der Massenkultur" in: Theodor W. Adorno, *Gesammelte Schriften*, vol. 3, ed. Rolf Tiedemann, Frankfurt am Main: Suhrkamp Verlag, 1997, p. 320.
34 | Christoph Schlingensief and Carl Hegemann, *Chance 2000: Wähle Dich selbst*, pp. 14-15.

for reflection and debate.³⁵ As I will explore in the following section, in *Quiz 3000* it is the nature of the questions posed to the contestants and, more specifically, their thematic difference from the kind of topics that ordinarily feature on such programs that generates the inconsistency in question.

## THE QUESTIONS

The first task (which appears, as do all subsequent questions, on screens that closely mimic the design format of *Who Wants to be a Millionaire?*) reads: "Order the following concentration camps from north to south! A: Auschwitz, B: Bergen-Belsen, C: Dachau, D: Ravensbrück."³⁶ The contestants (all of whom applied to appear on the program following a call for applications on the *Quiz 3000* website) scribble their answers furiously, hand them to Schlingensief's glamourously clad, high-heeled assistants who race across stage to form a line in anticipation of jury president Dietrich Kühlbrodt who inspects the answers to determine who will be the first to join Schlingensief at the spotlit table on stage. Kühlbrodt, who has appeared in many of Schlingensief's productions, also served as a Senior Public Prosecutor for Nazi crimes and is thus able to provide further context for the contestant/audience on topics pertaining to the Holocaust. For example, in response to the question – "What were the measurements of the standing cells at Auschwitz concentration camp in which four internees at a time had to spend the night?" –

---

**35** | See Alexander Kluge, "Das Halten von Totenschädeln liegt mir nicht/ Christoph Schlingensief inszeniert Hamlet", *News & Stories*, SAT 1, December 16, 2001. This discussion has been reproduced in Thekla Heineke and Sandra Umathum ed., *Christoph Schlingensiefs Nazis Rein*, Frankfurt am Main: Suhrkamp, 2002, p. 128.
**36** | This and a selection of other questions from the pilot version of the program can be accessed via the official *Quiz 3000* website: http://www.quiz3000.de/fragen16.3.pdf Last accessed November 1, 2014.

Kühlbrodt is able to confirm that "90 cm x 90cm" is, indeed, the correct answer and that internees were held in such cells for up to a week or even ten days at a time.

What is immediately apparent about these and other questions pertaining to the Holocaust is the degree to which they short-circuit the experience of pleasure associated with the contestant/audience member's capacity to answer the question. If, for example, in response to the query – "For what purpose was the hair that was shaved off the detainees in Auschwitz used for?" – the contestant is able to lock in the correct answer (ie."carpet and socks"), the sense of discomfort generated by the question, and by the memory of the camps and the inhumanity of the atrocities that occurred there, both outweighs the pleasure gained from providing the host with the correct answer and makes it very difficult for the contestant/audience member to proceed in an enthusiastic manner to the next question.

Figure 2: Quiz 3000. © Thomas Aurin

While only some of the questions focus directly on the Holocaust, throughout the program the contestants/viewers are confronted with questions in a similarly disturbing, albeit contemporary vein (a number of which, as I will explore in more detail, are connected in direct and/or tangential ways to the crimes committed by the Nazis):

Question: How many conscientious objectors from Kurdistan have, since 2001, been tortured to death in Turkey after being deported by Germany?

A. 3   B. 5   C. 7   D. 9

Answer: C


Question: The rape of members of which minority group is, according to the German criminal code, less heavily penalised?

A. Men   B. Animals   C. Children   D. People with disabilities

Answer: D


Question: By what percentage did the number of antisemitic motivated criminal offences rise in 2000 in contrast to the previous year?

A. 12 %.   B. 31%.   C. 55%.   D. 69%

Answer: D


What distinguishes these and other questions from those that feature on *Millionaire* is the degree to which their disturbing content disrupts the emphasis on immediate comprehension associated with information-oriented forms of communication that stunt the viewer's capacity to engage – in a reflective and autonomous manner – with the issues and ideas in question. As Benjamin makes clear, the "prime requirement" of information "is that it appear understandable in itself."[37] But what is "understandable" about forcing four people to stand overnight in a cell with a floor space of 90cm x 90cm? Why is the rape of disabled people less heavily penalised in Germany than the rape of other minority groups? And how is one to comprehend the German government's decision to deport Kurdish asylum seekers to Turkey given they knew, from past experience, there was a good chance they would be tortured and killed?

Instead of providing the contestants/viewers with a series of questions and answers that explain and/or pin meaning down, the answers provided by Schlingensief transform information into a catalyst for the kind of experience (*Erfahrung*) that Kluge associates with a realistic method because – in short-circuiting the passive mode of acceptance ordinarily associated with the presentation of facts as immutable – they compel the audience to challenge the realities with which they are presented and, in doing so, to continue the questioning process for themselves.

As mentioned previously, this questioning process is also set in motion by Schlingensief himself through discussions he instigates with the contestants about the issues and ideas at hand; conversations that, although very brief, provide a broader context within which the facts in question can be processed. For example, one of the questions posed to the contestant who went on to win the grand prize revolves around the average cost of fitting a prosthetic leg to victims of land mines. The contestant, who immigrated to Germany from the former Yugoslavia some thirty-three years before, undertakes humanitarian work raising money for victims of the Bosnian war. He has also campaigned against the use of land mines and thus knows from experience that the cost of fitting someone with a prosthetic leg is somewhere in the vicinity of 800 Euros. However, before the contestant's answer is revealed to be correct, Schlingensief initiates a discussion about the cost of land mines.

---

**37** | Walter Benjamin, "The Storyteller: Reflections on the Works of Nikolai Leskov" in: Walter Benjamin, Illuminations, ed. Hannah Arendt, London: Fontana Press, 1992, p. 88.

"One land mine", he states, "costs on average, I believe, around 1.80 Euro". The contestant, however, responds by noting that the land mines deployed in Bosnia were made in China and that they cost, back then, around 1.50 Deutschmark. Schlingensief notes that with the 10,000 Euros that the contestant has been nominally awarded, one could purchase a large number of land mines and then adds, before locking in the correct answer, that "the main producers of land mines are located in Germany and the USA". Later in the program, Germany's status as a major exporter of arms is again the topic of discussion; a conversation initiated by a question pertaining to the number of people killed in 2001 as a direct result of German-made weapons.

In contrast to the banter initiated by the host of *Millionaire?*, these discussions, although far from comprehensive, are (for this very reason) highly effective in encouraging the audience to become active participants in the meaning-making process because they function (in contrast to the mainstream news media) to ignite reflection rather than pin meaning down. "'You can learn nothing from the papers'", Benjamin notes by way of a story about his discussion with a sea captain:

'They always want to explain everything to you.' And in fact isn't it half the art of journalism to keep the news free from explanations? And didn't the ancients set an example for us by presenting events, as it were, dry, draining them of psychological explanations and opinions of every sort?[38]

For Schlingensief, as for Benjamin, it is clear that the information driven focus of news reports functions to delimit, rather than stimulate understanding; a point emphasised by one of the *Quiz 3000* contestants who, when asked by Schlingensef whether she is certain that she has locked in the correct answer, states: "I can't be sure because .[..] we don't experience [*erfahren*] anything from our media". This statement is immediately corroborated by one of sev-

---

**38** | Walter Benjamin, "The Handkerchief" in *Walter Benjamin, Selected Writings: Volume 2*, pp. 659-660.

eral image montages that are projected – at different points in the program – on the back wall of the *Quiz 3000* stage. The montage in question, which functions to both draw attention to – and *enact* – the degree of desensitisation that occurs when images of war, terror, violence, and destruction are packaged as information for public consumption, consists of a rapidly edited collection of television news footage. We see (among other images) snippets of George W. Bush and Gerhard Schröder pointing in unison at the camera; we watch footage of the World Trade Centre Towers collapsing; and we see a coffin draped in the German flag. Images of corpses scattered on the ground flit by as do faces of people imprisoned behind barbed wire; images of Saddam Hussein and Osama Bin Laden flash up and disappear just as rapidly, as does footage of television news anchors, military hardware, and soldiers with guns.

The second montage (which appears some ten minutes later) consists of footage pertaining to Adolf Hitler, National Socialism, and the Holocaust. This sequence (which is edited at a much slower pace) opens with the image of a giant swastika, marching soldiers, and crowds saluting Hitler. It is followed by black and white footage of planes dropping bombs, people being executed, barbed wire, piles of corpses, and human beings reduced to walking skeletons. In contrast to the previous montage (the rapid pace of which enacts the anaesthetising effects that Benjamin associates with an information-driven news culture), the second montage encourages viewers to reflect on, and to *feel*, the reality of the atrocities that constitute the information-driven statistics in question.

It is clear that by juxtaposing contemporary news footage with footage of the Holocaust and the second world war, Schlingensief is also asking viewers to reflect on whether the barbarism characteristic of the Third Reich does, in fact, belong solely to the past, or whether its traces can be found in certain sectors of the media and political culture of the twenty-first century in Germany, the USA, and elsewhere. As Schlingensief himself has made clear in a discussion about his film *100 Jahre Adolf Hitler* that is true of his work on history and politics more generally: "It wasn't about some historical psychic profile, not about unmasking. Rather it was about delusion here and now, about the ghosts of the *Führer*, the muck in ourselves".[39]

In *Quiz 3000*, this "delusion" and "muck" emerges (through a suggestive rather than didactic process) as a result of questions that prompt the contestant/viewer to reflect on the actuality of the Nazi legacy. For example, while the question concerning the rise in anti-semitic violence is explicit in drawing attention to the connections between Germany's past and present, other questions pertaining to the deportation of Kurdish asylum seekers and the legal consequences of the rape of disabled people ask the contestant/viewer to consider why the lives of some human beings are judged to be more valuable than others and, furthermore, to what degree a relationship of continuity exists between Nazi policies on disability, for example, and decisions that are made in contemporary political and legal spheres.

It is this questioning process, and the active, autonomous mode of reflection with which it is associated, that aligns the spectatorial relationship cultivated by *Quiz 3000* with the mode of experience that Benjamin describes as *Erfahrung* in which thought is provoked, in part, by the amalgamation of the past and the present. In fact, one could extrapolate on Schlingensief's criticism of the information-driven displays at Dachau and argue that what is problematic for Schlingensief about such exhibits is the degree to which, to quote Benjamin, they provide "the object [or incident] with a classificatory number behind which it disappears".[40] As a result, the viewer is left with the impression that these horrific acts of violence and destruc-

---

**39** | Schlingensief, *Ich weiß, ich war's*, ed. Aino Laberenz, Köln: Kiepenheuer & Witsch, 2012, p. 229.

**40** | Walter Benjamin, *The Arcades Project*, H5, 1, p. 211. For Schlingensief's analysis of the degree to which this kind of "memory culture" situates the spectator in a relationship of distance to the past, see *Ich weiß, ich war's*, pp. 227-8.

tion are the product of a bygone, barbaric past and, therefore, bear little if any relationship to the now of the "civilized" present.

In contrast, *Quiz 3000* encourages viewers to adopt a perspective that reflects on and questions the twenty-first century continuation of a certain Fascistic logic according to which the destruction of lives is represented as an "unfortunate" byproduct of the march of progress enacted by powerful nations seeking to shore up their power, accumulate wealth, fortify "freedom", and secure their national borders. This is not to suggest that Schlingensief's work is driven by a desire to relativise the Holocaust. Rather, what *Quiz 3000* does do is encourage contestants/viewers to ask, among other questions, why Germany – which is responsible for the piles of corpses depicted in the montage described above – is one of the largest international producers and exporters of military arms; to reflect on why a country which had a policy of "euthanizing" disabled people continues to discriminate against people with disabilities; and to question why anti-Semitic violence is on the rise in a country that has sought to atone for, and move on from, the crimes of the past.

In contrast, however, to quiz shows such as *Who Wants to be a Millionaire?*, it is clearly not Schlingensief's intention to provide the audience with clear-cut answers on these and other matters. Rather, as the questions cited above make clear, the answers that Schlingensief *does* provide function to open up, rather than close meaning down; to frustrate the emphasis on easy comprehension that Benjamin associates with *Erlebnis*; and to encourage the viewer to draw both on their own experience – and the experience garnered from the mistakes of the past – in an attempt to grapple with a status quo that is marked, in part, by inequality, unhappiness, and oppression.

In stark contrast to the "matter-of-fact" approach of the news media described by Benjamin, Kluge argues that "[t]he root of a realistic attitude, its motivation" is not the confirmation of a certain reality or truth but rather *"opposition* to the misery present in real circumstances". "[I]t is", he writes, "therefore, an anti-Realism of motivation, a denial of the pure reality-principle, an *anti-realistic attitude* which alone enables one to look realistically and attentively".[41] By re-enacting *Who Wants to be a Millionaire?*, Schlingensief not only undermined the "reality-principle" governing the information-driven focus of both quiz shows and the mainstream news media. Rather, he demonstrated – in a most compelling way – the significant role that a realistic re-enactment of reality television can play as a catalyst for experience, reflection, and political debate.

---

**41** | Alexander Kluge, "The Political as Intensity of Everyday Feeling" in: *Alexander Kluge: Raw Materials For the Imagination*, ed. Tara Forrest, Amsterdam: Amsterdam University Press, 2012, p. 284.

# CHAPTER 6

A Negative Utopia:

Haneke's Fragmentary Cinema

> [T]he history of film contains a utopian strain – which is what accounts for the attraction of the cinema – but it is a utopia which, contrary to the Greek meaning of *ou-topos* = no place, is in existence *everywhere* and especially in the *unsophisticated* imagination. This unsophisticated imagination, however, is buried under a thick layer of cultural garbage. It has to be dug out. This project of excavation, not at all a utopian notion, can be realized only through our work.
>
> ALEXANDER KLUGE[1]

In reviews of his work, Michael Haneke is often described as a pessimistic director whose films present us with a bleak, dystopian outlook on the possibilities of the world in which we live.[2] In interviews,

---

**1** | Alexander Kluge, "On Film and the Public Sphere" in: *Alexander Kluge: Raw Materials For the Imagination*, ed. Tara Forrest, Amsterdam: Amsterdam University Press, 2012, p. 37.

**2** | Robin Wood, for example, has described Haneke as "perhaps the most pessimistic of all great filmmakers", Monisha Rajesh refers to the "trademark nihilism" characteristic of his work, and Claudia Puig states that Haneke has an "unrelentingly nihilistic world view". See Robin Wood, "Hidden in plain

however, Haneke reacts vehemently to such claims stating that his films are in fact utopian, albeit in a negative sense, because the grim scenarios they represent challenge the audience to conceive of the degree to which things could, in fact, be very different. "If", Haneke states, "there is a Utopia for me, that is worthy of its name, it can only be a negative one – a utopia that mobilises powers of resistance".[3]

Although this concept of negative utopianism could be explored in relation to Haneke's oeuvre more generally[4], focusing on his 1994 film *71 Fragments of a Chronology of Chance* (*71 Fragmente einer Chronologie des Zufalls*), this chapter will examine how – and with what effects – its experimental form could be seen to "mobilise[...] powers of resistance" against the alienated image of reality presented on screen. Drawing on the ideas of Kluge, Adorno, and Benjamin, I will argue that – far from being dystopian – *71 Fragments* encourages the audience to think critically and imaginatively about the extent to which life could be transformed for the better.

---

sight: Robin Wood on Michael Haneke's Cache", *Artforum International*, Vol. 44, No. 5 (January, 2006), p. 35, Monisha Rajesh, "Michael Haneke's Film Noir", *Time* (November 30, 2009), and Claudia Puig, "Elegant 'White Ribbon' gets all tied up in monotonous gloom", *USA Today* (January 8, 2010).

3 | Thomas Assheuer and Michael Haneke, *Nahaufnahme Michael Haneke. Gespräche mit Thomas Assheuer*, Berlin: Alexander Verlag, 2008, p. 133. See also Haneke's comments on this topic in Stefan Grissemann and Michael Omasta, "Herr Haneke, wo bleibt das Positive?" in *Der Siebente Kontinent: Michael Haneke und seine Filme*, ed. Alexander Horwath, Wien and Zürich: Europaverlag, 1991, p. 203.

4 | This concept has not, to my knowledge, been explored in any detail in relation to Haneke's work. See, however, Kevin L. Stoehr's very brief analysis of Haneke as an "anti-nihilist" in "Haneke's Secession: Perspectivisim and Anti-Nihilism in *Code Unknown and Caché*" in: *A Companion to Michael Haneke*, ed. Roy Grundmann, Malden and Oxford: Wiley-Blackwell, 2010, pp. 489-491. Stoehr does not, however, discuss the idea of negative utopianism.

## Negative Utopianism

In an interview with Thomas Assheuer that took place in 2007, Haneke's interest in the productive effects of negative utopianism are revealed in a discussion about his early work in the theatre. Reflecting on a production of Friedrich Hebbel's *Maria Magdalena* which he directed in Germany some thirty years ago, Haneke recalls a heated, post-premiere discussion he had with a senior dramaturge, who was also a student of Adorno. As Haneke makes clear, what troubled the dramaturge about the production (which, for Haneke, was a great success) was the sense of "hopelessness" and "complete lack of utopia" characteristic of his staging of the play. "*What*", Assheur asks Haneke,

*did you say in response to him?*

That one has to fight against the production and the play and that Adorno himself surely would have understood that.

*On account of the compelling aesthetic form?*

On account of the form. What would the alternative be? Should art convey utopia, a message directly? Who is supposed to take that seriously? Only through the negation of utopia does the recipient have the opportunity to say no and to fight against it.[5]

As Haneke's comments both here and elsewhere suggest, this negative conception of utopia is, in part, indebted to Adorno's analysis of the important role that art can play in challenging the limited, affirmative image of reality propagated by the culture industry. Utopia, Adorno states, can only be found "in the determined negation of that which merely is, and by concretizing itself as something false,

---

**5** | Assheuer and Haneke, *Nahaufnahme Michael Haneke. Gespräche mit Thomas Assheuer*, p. 100.

it always points at the same time to what should be."⁶ Utopia, in this sense, is manifested in the "determined negation" of that which is wrong, that which is morally reprehensible, and that which is rendered false because it threatens the potential for a world free from domination, suffering and despair. According to Adorno, "determined negation" thus becomes the praxis through which the possibility of a different reality may be actualised.⁷

Within this schema, it is therefore neither the role of the artist nor the filmmaker to represent "what should be" in a concrete way. While "there is", Adorno states, "nothing like a single, fixable utopian content"⁸, the role of the artist/filmmaker is to rejuvenate the viewer's capacity for imagination and to encourage him/her to reflect on the degree to which the world could be transformed for the better. While the contours of this world are not, according to Adorno, some-

---

**6** | Ernst Bloch and Theodor W. Adorno, "Something's Missing: A Discussion between Ernst Bloch and Theodor W. Adorno on the Contradictions of Utopian Longing" in: Ernst Bloch, *The Utopian Function of Art and Literature: Selected Essays*, Cambridge and London: The MIT Press, 1988, p. 12.

**7** | See also Geoff Boucher's summary of Adorno's position which is evocative of Haneke's approach. "The utopian impulse in contemporary thinking", he writes, "must not be lost. Adorno's concern with reconciliation in modernist artworks springs fundamentally from his affirmation of the importance of human happiness. In the context of a problematic development of modernity, this means a principled defence of the right of suffering to have a voice, for in the expression of indignation at injustice, Adorno detects the desire for utopia". Geoff Boucher, *Adorno Reframed*, London: IB Tauris, 2013, p. 152. "[C]onsumate negativity", Adorno writes, "delineates the mirror image of its opposite". Theodor Adorno, *Minima Moralia: Reflections from Damaged Life*, London: Verso, 1974, p. 247.

**8** | Bloch and Adorno, "Something's Missing: A Discussion between Ernst Bloch and Theodor W. Adorno on the Contradictions of Utopian Longing", p. 7.

thing that can be pre-drawn[9], it is clear that the utopia he invokes is both free from domination and organised, in part, around the minimisation of suffering and the maximisation of happiness, freedom and human potential.[10] However, as both Adorno and Haneke make clear, instead of presenting the viewer with a "message", or with a utopian image of the world as an ideal place, the primary aim of negative utopianism is to facilitate a desire for change. "[T]he true thing", Adorno states,

determines itself via the false thing, or via that which makes itself falsely known. And insofar as we are not allowed to cast the picture of utopia, insofar as we do not know what the correct thing would be, we know exactly, to be sure, what the false thing is. That is actually the only form in which utopia is given to us at all.[11]

As discussed in previous chapters, for Kluge, film's ability to facilitate change is intimately bound with its capacity to stimulate the imagination of the audience. What troubles him about the mass media (he cites conventional narrative films and television news programs as examples) is the degree to which the image of reality they represent actively shapes our understanding of what is and isn't possible and impacts negatively on our capacity to conceive of the degree to which things could, in fact, be very different. For Adorno, too, it is the standardised products of the culture industry (in the form of films, television programs, and popular music) that are "infecting

---

**9** | For an analysis of the degree to which Adorno's thinking in this regard has been influenced by the Jewish ban on images, see Adriana S. Benzaquén, "Thought and Utopia in the Writings of Adorno, Horkheimer and Benjamin", *Utopian Studies*, Vol. 9, No. 2 (1998).

**10** | See Adorno's comments in this regard in Bloch and Adorno, "Something's Missing: A Discussion between Ernst Bloch and Theodor W. Adorno on the Contradictions of Utopian Longing", p. 7.

**11** | Ibid., p. 12.

everything with sameness".¹² "The procedure", he writes, "follows the basic culture-industrial principle: affirmation of life as it is".¹³

If Haneke, too, is troubled by the standardised, affirmative character of the mainstream media, it is because of the negative impact it has on the audience's capacity to think critically and imaginatively about the ideas, values, and prejudices that actively shape the world in which we live. "People", Haneke states,

> can no longer bear ambivalences. Why? Because they have become so used to it from television and mainstream dramaturgy. They only know narrative forms that answer all their questions so that they are able to go home feeling pacified. That is what they pay for. [...] That is a type of commercialisation of our understanding of reality that I don't want to accept.¹⁴

This reference to the mainstream media's "commercialisation of our understanding of reality" can be read on at least two different – albeit interrelated – levels. In a very general sense, it refers to the role that the mass media (in the form of advertising, film, and television) play in the representation and idealization of a particular image of "reality" according to which the value and success of one's life are determined by one's capacity to purchase certain products. As Adorno outlines in his "Prologue to Television", by equating a happy, fulfilled life with the "fortunes of the department store", the commercially driven "utopia" generated by the mainstream media

---

12 | Horkheimer, Max and Theodor W. Adorno, *Dialectic of Englightenment: Philosophical Fragments*, Stanford: Stanford UP, 2002, p. 94.

13 | Theodor W. Adorno, *Introduction to the Sociology of Music*, New York: Continuum, 1989, p. 37.

14 | Assheuer and Haneke, *Nahaufnahme Michael Haneke. Gespräche mit Thomas Assheuer*, p. 130. See also Kluge's television interview with Haneke in which the latter draws a distinction between a film practice which generates contradictions and one which merely "shows". "Die rechte Hand Gottes: Michael Haneke über seinen preisgekrönten Film *Das Weisse Band*", *News & Stories* (November 1, 2009).

functions to "extirpate the idea of utopia from human beings altogether and to make them swear their allegiance all the more deeply to the established order".[15]

In relation to the specific concerns of this chapter, this commercialisation process is also manifested in the passive, non-participatory mode of engagement fostered by the mainstream media and the "products" it produces. As Adorno writes in "The Schema of Mass Culture", it is "the pre-digested quality of the product [that] prevails".[16] By generating images, narratives, and ideas that reinforce audience expectations (expectations that have, in large part, been shaped by the culture industry itself) Adorno argues that mainstream media products cultivate a mode of engagement that requires little effort on behalf of the spectator because "the message is invariably that of identification with the status quo".[17] Put simply, the viewer, in this context, becomes a consumer because he/she is able to swallow the "premasticated" products whole.[18]

Within this schema, Haneke's outline for an alternative filmmaking practice is driven by a desire to shake up the commercial image of reality generated by the mainstream media and, in doing so, to undermine the passive, consumer-oriented mode of engagement that he associates with both mainstream television programs and Hollywood cinema. "My films", he states,

---

**15** | Theodor W. Adorno, "Prologue to Television" in *Critical Models: Interventions and Catchwords*, New York and Chichester: Columbia University Press, 1998, p. 57.
**16** | Theodor W. Adorno, "The Schema of Mass Culture" in: *The Culture Industry: Selected Essays on Mass Culture*, ed. J.M. Bernstein, London and New York: Routledge, 1991, p. 67.
**17** | Theodor W. Adorno, "Transparencies on Film" in: *The Culture Industry: Selected Essays on Mass Culture*, London and New York: Routledge, 1991, p. 164.
**18** | Adorno, *Introduction to the Sociology of Music*, p. 30.

should provide a countermodel to the typically American style of total production to be found in contemporary popular cinema, which, in its hermetically sealed illusion of an ultimately intact reality, deprives the spectator of any possibility of critical participation and condemns him from the outset to the role of a simple consumer.[19]

It is this emphasis on generating an active, participatory mode of engagement that is the driving force behind the production of 71 *Fragments* and that aligns Haneke's delineation of the possibilities of the medium with Kluge's analysis of the "utopian strain" of cinema. As his comments in the epigraph make clear, for Kluge the utopian promise of film lies not in its capacity to present us with an ideal image of an alternate reality, but in its ability to disinter the spectator's capacity for imagination from the "thick layer of cultural garbage" under which it is buried. The audience, in this context, is not invited to passively immerse themselves in another world, but to reflect on the shortcomings of the reality on screen and, in the process, imagine how life could, in reality, be transformed. Haneke describes this mode of engagement as a form of "resistance" because instead of consuming the film "whole", the audience is prompted by the experimental form of 71 *Fragments* to reflect critically on the society in which the characters live – a society which is permeated by so much suffering, alienation, and despair. As Adriana S. Benzaquén has stated in her analysis of Adorno's work, it is "the reality of suffering [in this case, depicted on screen, that] testifies to the possibility *and* necessity of change".[20]

For both Haneke and Kluge, it is only by fragmenting the film's narrative and, in the process, undermining the passive mode of engagement that they associate with the "intact reality" generated by conventional narrative cinema that the audience is "jolt[ed] ... out of

---

**19** | Amos Vogel, "Of Nonexisting Continents: The Cinema of Michael Haneke", *Film Comment*, Vol. 32, No. 4 (July/August, 1996), p. 75.
**20** | Benzaquén, "Thought and Utopia in the Writings of Adorno, Horkheimer and Benjamin", p. 152.

their attitude of consumerism"[21] and encouraged to actively participate in the meaning-making process. In a similar vein to Bertolt Brecht's analysis of the active, critical mode of engagement cultivated by the "radical *separation of the elements*" characteristic of Epic Theatre[22], Kluge argues that film "is not produced by *auteurs* alone, but by the dialogue between spectators and authors"[23] – a dialogue that is not manifested in the film itself, but in the thoughts and connections cultivated in "the spectator's head" by "the gaps [...] between the disparate elements of filmic expression".[24]

As I will discuss in more detail in the following sections, it is the open, experimental form of *71 Fragments* – combined with Haneke's extensive use of long takes and his predilection for truncating action and dialogue – that facilitates a genuinely cooperative, communicative relationship between the audience and the film. As will become clear, it is this active, participatory mode of engagement (and not the narrative content of *71 Fragments*) that constitutes the utopian promise of the film.

### Communication that doesn't communicate

*71 Fragments* is the third work in a series of films that is often described as the "trilogy of glaciation" following Haneke's claim that the films are "reports on the progression of the emotional glacia-

---

**21** | Michael Haneke, "*71 Fragments of a Chronology of Chance: Notes to the Film*" in: *After Postmodernism: Austrian Literature and Film in Transition*, ed. Willy Riemer, Riverside: Ariadne Press, 2000, p. 174.
**22** | Bertolt Brecht, "The Modern Theatre is the Epic Theatre" in: *Brecht on Theatre: The Development of an Aesthetic*, ed. John Willett, New York: Hill and Wang, 1998, p. 37.
**23** | Jan Dawson, '"But Why are the Questions so Abstract?': An Interview with Alexander Kluge" in: Jan Dawson, *Alexander Kluge and the Occasional Work of a Female Slave*, Zoetrope, New York, p. 37.
**24** | Edgar Reitz, Alexander Kluge and Wilfried Reinke, "Word and Film", *October*, 46 (Fall, 1988), p. 87.

tion" of Austria.²⁵ In keeping with the other films that constitute the trilogy²⁶, *71 Fragments* is populated by lonely, alienated characters who are emotionally detached from the world in which they live. Among the key characters are: a young, homeless Romanian boy who has travelled to Vienna in the back of a truck because he has heard that Austrians "are nice to children"; a lonely, elderly man who spends most of his time in front of the television set and who has a difficult relationship with his bank-teller daughter; a rogue member of the armed forces who steals and trades in military weapons; a couple who are seeking to adopt a young girl who rejects their attempts at familial communication; a university student named Maximilian who is also a table-tennis player; and a middle-aged security officer whose relationship to his wife is strained to the absolute limit. As the title suggests, the film itself is constructed out of seventy-one fragments that provide us with partial, interrupted access to the day-to-day activities of this disconnected, largely nameless group of characters whose lives intersect by chance – and with disastrous consequences – at the end of the film.

Haneke has started that the trilogy is "about the topic of communication that doesn't communicate" and it is clear that the characters who populate *71 Fragments* find it extremely difficult to connect and communicate with each other in a satisfactory and meaningful way. For example, in a scene that takes place at the zoo, we view the couple with Anni (the young girl whom they are seeking to adopt) as they watch the animated performance of the seals as they participate in their feeding-time ritual. While the couple and the girl appear to be enjoying the performance, the laughter of the former is somewhat forced and it is clear that these prospective parents are more interested in generating the appearance of familial fun, rather

---

**25** | Michael Haneke, "Film als Katharsis" in: *Austria (in)felix: zum österreichischen Film der 80er Jahre*, ed. Francesco Bono, Graz: Edition Blimp, 1992, p. 89.

**26** | These include *The Seventh Continent* (1989) and *Benny's Video* (1992).

than relaxing and enjoying the experience for what it is. When the woman, however, puts her arm around Anni's shoulders, both the "fun" and the scene are abruptly brought to a halt by Anni's cold, angry expression and by her prompt rejection of the woman's hasty, somewhat stilted attempt at affection.

*Figure 1: 71 Fragments of a Chronology of Chance*

Haneke's emphasis on the difficult, forced nature of interpersonal relations is also made clearly apparent in scenes that revolve around the elderly man and his bank-teller daughter. In an early scene at the bank, we view the daughter going through the motions of customer service, only to find out at the end of the transaction that the customer is in fact her father. "I don't", she states, "have any time now Father. Call in the evening and we can talk". When her father, however, follows her instructions, the call that ensues is frosty and awkward. In a scene that consists of one still, long take that lasts for more than eight minutes, we view the father on the phone in his flat and imagine the daughter at the other end of the line participating begrudgingly in a conversation with a father whom she views – as the elderly man himself points out – as an irritating and tiresome burden.

This lack – but also suspicion – of familial warmth is, however, communicated most disturbingly in the film in a scene between the security guard and his wife who are eating dinner at the family table. When the security guard/husband interrupts the silence with an awkward, softly spoken "I love you", his wife is shocked and suspicious and immediately asks him if he is drunk. When the husband responds in the affirmative, she becomes angry and questions what he wants, noting that it isn't something that one says "out of the blue". Frustrated by his wife's comments and by his own unwillingness and/or inability to answer her questions, he slaps her violently in the face. After a moment's pause, however, the woman reaches out and touches his arm in a gesture of reconciliation, and they continue – albeit in an uncomfortable silence – eating their dinner at the table.

Although, as these examples make clear, the film is very much concerned with exploring what Haneke views as a breakdown in interpersonal communication, on another level, *71 Fragments* also interrogates the role that the mass media plays – on a much broader scale – in stunting, rather than facilitating, communication. Television screens and news broadcasts feature regularly in Haneke's films, especially in *71 Fragments* which begins and ends with a montage of clips from a series of television news broadcasts. These clips (which also appear throughout the course of the film) provide us with access to footage from stories that were broadcast between October and December in 1993, and that focus on events such as: the Bosnian war; an IRA bomb attack in Belfast; a strike by Air France workers; a PKK terrorist attack in Eastern Anatolia; an address by Michael Jackson following allegations of child abuse; the UN war crimes tribunal for atrocities committed in former Yugoslavia; an Israeli attack on southern Lebanon; and a shooting spree in a bank in Vienna undertaken by a university student. As will be explored in more detail in the following sections, the latter story is also reenacted in the film and serves both as the culmination point of Haneke's fictional account of events that led up to the shooting, and the site at which the lives of the various characters in the film intersect.

*Figure 2: 71 Fragments of a Chronology of Chance*

What troubles Haneke about television news programs is the degree to which their pace, organization, and narrative structure distance and – in the process – anaesthetise viewers from the issues and events depicted on screen and, in doing so, further contribute to what he describes as the "emotional glaciation" of the spectator. For Haneke, this glaciation process is very much a modern phenomenon. He argues that, prior to the development of the mass media, knowledge of the world was limited to one's "immediate environment" and thus "nourished by [...one's] direct experience"[27]. Today, he states "[w]e live in this environment where we think we know more things faster, when in fact we know nothing at all".[28] Drawing on the cave allegory outlined in Plato's *The Republic*[29], Haneke argues that our distant, heavily mediated relationship to the world around us is comparable to the experience of the prisoners described in Plato's story who mis-

---

**27** | Assheuer and Haneke, *Nahaufnahme Michael Haneke. Gespräche mit Thomas Assheuer*, p. 55.
**28** | Christopher Sharrett, "The World That is Known: An Interview with Michael Haneke", *Cineaste* (Summer, 2003), p. 31.
**29** | Plato, *The Republic*, London: Penguin, 1987, pp. 316-25.

take the shadows projected on the wall of the cave in which they are imprisoned for reality itself.[30] As Haneke makes clear:

> What we know of the world is little more than the mediated world, the image. We have no reality, but a derivative of reality, which is extremely dangerous, most certainly from a political standpoint but also in a larger sense to [sic] our ability to have a palpable sense of the truth of everyday experience.[31]

This emphasis on the diminution in the capacity for communication and experience cultivated, in part, by the mass media resonates strongly with Walter Benjamin's analysis of the modern decline in the "communicability of experience" that he associates with the rise of an information culture.[32] Central to Benjamin's analysis of the growth of information as a means of communication is the decline in the art of storytelling and the communicability of experience with which he associates it. For Benjamin, what is significant about storytelling is the degree to which the storyteller is able to recount a tale in such a way that its meaning is not communicated to the listener directly. In a manner which anticipates Haneke's delineation of the task of a fragmentary film practice, Benjamin argues that "it is half the art of storytelling to keep a story free from explanation as one reproduces it".[33] "The most extraordinary things, marvellous things", he writes, "are related with the greatest accuracy, but the psychological connection of the events is

---

**30** | See, for example, Haneke's comments in Assheuer and Haneke, *Nahaufnahme Michael Haneke. Gespräche mit Thomas Assheuer*, p. 55.
**31** | Sharrett, "The World That is Known: An Interview with Michael Haneke", p. 30.
**32** | Walter Benjamin, "The Storyteller: Reflections on the Works of Nikolai Leskov" in: Walter Benjamin, *Illuminations*, ed. Hannah Arendt, London: Fontana Press, 1992, p. 86.
**33** | Benjamin, "The Storyteller: Reflections on the Works of Nikolai Leskov", p. 89.

not forced on the reader".³⁴ Rather, the tale is recounted in a manner that prompts the listener to draw on his/her own experience and imagination in an attempt to fill out the contours of the story.

For Haneke, too, it is the emphasis placed by the mass media (he cites television news programs and Hollywood cinema as examples) on presenting the viewer with rapidly edited, "pre-digested" bites of information that stunt our capacity to experience the images on screen. "Contemporary film editing", he notes, "is most commonly determined by practices of TV-timing, by the expectation of a rapid flow of information [...] which can be quickly consumed and checked off".³⁵ While information as a mode of communication can, in this sense, be easily registered, the mixed structure and rapid pace characteristic, for example, of television news programs stunts the audience's capacity to participate in the meaning-making process because the viewer is left with scant opportunity to reflect on the issues, ideas, and events at hand. "Television", Haneke states, "accelerates experience, but one needs time to understand what one sees, which the current media disallows".³⁶

---

34 | Ibid. "The value of information", he writes, "does not survive the moment in which it was new. It lives only at the moment; it has to surrender to it completely and explain itself to it without losing any time. A story is different. It does not expend itself. It preserves and concentrates its strength and is capable of releasing it even after a long time". See pp. 89-90.
35 | Haneke quoted in Catherine Wheatley, *Michael Haneke's Cinema: The Ethic of the Image*, New York: Berghahn Books, 2009, p. 72.
36 | Sharrett, "The World That is Known: An Interview with Michael Haneke", p. 31. Negt and Kluge argue in a similar vein that "[i]n taking on an increasingly abstract character, the news items turn into entertainment. Brief reports about fatal accidents do not cause a stir. If they are summed up on the evening news (for example, 87 dead in a plane crash, 500 Vietcong killed, the deaths of an elderly president and a famous scientist, two fatal car accidents), they assume the abstract nature of a body count, of a mere recording of casualites. It is impossible to get news items of this kind across unless one succeeds in stimulating in the viewer a sensual impression of the underlying

As I will explore in more detail in the following section, if the spectatorial effects generated by the open, experimental form of *71 Fragments* differ from the mode of engagement fostered by the fragmentary structure, rapid pace, and information driven content of television news programs, it is in part because the comparatively slow, meditative pace of Haneke's film provides the viewer with the opportunity to reflect on (rather than to simply register) the images and events on screen: to question the characters' motivations and the priorities of the society in which they live; and to think critically about what would need to change for life to be transformed into something very different. In a manner that resonates strongly with Benjamin's delineation of the storyteller's practice (within which the content and meaning of the tale are not communicated to the listener directly), Haneke argues that "[a] film's essential feature, its criterion of quality, should be its ability to become the productive centre of an interactive process".[37]

### The Film in the Spectator's Head

> It is not the office of art to spotlight alternatives, but to resist by its form alone the course of the world, which permanently puts a pistol to men's heads.
> THEODOR W. ADORNO[38]

human tragedies. For this purpose, real history would have to be told, for it alone constitutes news." Oskar Negt and Alexander Kluge, *Public Sphere and Experience: Toward an Analysis of the Bourgeois and Proletarian Public Sphere*, pp. 119-20. See also Kluge's criticism of the form of television news broadcasts in Alexander Kluge, "The Moment of Tragic Recognition with a Happy Ending" in: *The Power of Intellectuals in Contemporary Germany*, ed. Michael Geyer, Chicago and London: University of Chicago Press, 2001, pp. 386-7.

**37** | Haneke, *"71 Fragments of a Chronology of Chance:* Notes to the Film", p. 171.

**38** | Theodor Adorno, "Commitment" in: Theodor Adorno, Walter Benjamin, Ernst Bloch, Bertolt Brecht and Georg Lukacs, *Aesthetics and Politics*, London and New York: Verso, 1990, p. 180.

*71 Fragments* opens with a black screen with white text that recounts in a clipped, journalistic style an event that took place in Vienna in 1993: "On 23. 12. 93 in the branch office of a Viennese bank, 19 year old student Maximilian B. shot three people and killed himself shortly afterwards with a shot in the head". This intertitle is immediately followed by a clip from a television news program which aired on October 12, 1993 and which contains three reports that focus on, among other issues, occurrences, and events: people fleeing war in Abkhazia; a US military attack in Somalia; and the tension generated by the presence of US warship Harlan County in Port-au-Prince. While the first and third news reports appear in truncated form, in a similar vein to the information contained in the intertitle, the style of the reports is very clipped, and the audience is provided with scant opportunity to understand or engage with the issues at hand.

In the first report about Abkhazia, for example, we are presented with images of weapons lighting up the night sky. This footage is quickly followed by images of people walking in a long line. The man at the front of the group is holding a piece of white cloth and the voiceover states (before shifting gear to a report about Somalia): "With a handkerchief as a peace flag, the people walk through the firing lines. There are still more than one hundred thousand people fleeing the war". What is missing, however, from the report is the kind of context that would enable viewers to get a sense of the background and issues that led up to – or served as catalysts for – these events. Weapons (which, of course, have very real effects on their targets) are aestheticised as streaks of light in the sky, and while the people on screen are immediately recognisable as victims of war, the fast-paced, information driven content of the report not only prohibits us from learning anything about their story, but provides us with little insight into what it would be like to experience such terror.

When, at the end of the film, Haneke reenacts the story about the shooting described in the opening intertitle, it is with the aim of undermining the detached, consumer-oriented mode of engagement cultivated by the information-driven focus of such reports; the structure and pace of which leave the viewer feeling "informed" but without any investment in – or sense of connection to – the issues and events in question. The reenactment scene is, in itself, quite brief: We view the security guard as he moves through the bank with an armoured briefcase. As he walks toward the exit, we recognise the woman who was seeking to adopt Anni (but who has, in the meantime, chosen instead to take care of the young Romanian immigrant) as she participates in a conversation with a bank-teller. We also notice the lonely, elderly man in the queue and we can see his bank-teller daughter behind the counter. As the security guard prepares to exit the bank, Maximilian enters with his gun held high and immediately fires shots into the crowd. We hear the screams of the people in the bank, and then we view the student in an overhead shot that follows his movements as he crosses the road and enters his car, which is parked in a busy service station. The shot rests on the overhead image of his vehicle, a gunshot rings out, and the fragment cuts to black.

In contrast to the news report described above, these violent acts are certainly not aestheticised, and the camera follows the events as they unfold in a cool, distant, almost scientific manner that is characteristic of the style of the film as a whole.[39] Our relationship, however, to these random, horrific acts of violence is anything but distanced or detached. Unlike the people who feature in the news reports that intersperse the film, we are very familiar with the characters in (and their relatives outside) the bank whose lives will be disastrously impacted by the shooting. Although we view Maximilian firing into the crowd, Haneke refrains from providing us with any shorthand information about the consequences of his actions. The fragment thus generates what Benjamin describes as "an ampli-

---

**39** | In interviews, Haneke often expresses his aversion to films that aestheticise violence in order to render it palatable for the viewer. See, for example, Franz Grabner, '"Der Name der Erbsünde ist Verdrängung': Ein Gespräch mit Michael Haneke" in: *Michael Haneke und seine Filme: Eine Pathologie der Konsumgesellschaft*, ed. Christian Wessely, Gerhard Larcher, and Franz Grabner, Marburg: Schüren Verlag, 2005, pp. 36-7.

tude that information lacks"⁴⁰ because the audience is encouraged to imagine how Maximilian's actions will change the lives of these characters whom we have followed throughout the film and who have already experienced so much unhappiness.

When, at the end of the film, we are presented with an actual news report about the shooting that was broadcast on Austrian television, we engage with the material on screen in a manner that differs from the distant, detached mode of engagement ordinarily facilitated by television news programs because, in this instance, we are able to fill in the human details that are occluded by the information-driven content of the report. While we learn, for example, that the attack took place in Billrothstraße and that three people were killed as a result, when the voiceover states that the motive for the attack is "completely unclear", we beg to differ – not because the shooting is in any way justified, but because we are aware of the deep sense of human disconnectedness, alienation, and loneliness experienced not only by Maximilian, but also by the other characters who populate the film. As Haneke has stated in relation to the acts of violence committed in the trilogy:

The real horror about them [...] is the suspicion that the supposedly irrational acts could have altogether rationally discoverable roots in our life style. This horror is dramaturgically productive. It makes it possible to have the spectators confront themselves, since they are forced to look for the answers which the film and its plot fail to give.[41]

This active, participatory mode of engagement is cultivated by the film on a number of different levels – all of which encourage the spectator to become creative co-producers in the meaning-making process: to resist, rather than consume, the bleak image of society

---

**40** | Benjamin, "The Storyteller: Reflections on the Works of Nikolai Leskov", p. 89.
**41** | Haneke, "*71 Fragments of a Chronology of Chance:* Notes to the Film", p. 174.

depicted on screen; and to imagine how life could – in reality – be transformed into something very different. Foremost among the devices employed by Haneke to this effect is the experimental form of the film itself which, as noted previously, consists of seventy-one fragments separated from each other by cuts to black and that are organised in a chronological, albeit open and ambiguous manner. Many of the fragments themselves also appear in truncated form with sentences, actions, and gestures cut off prematurely: a highly effective device that works to open up, rather than close meaning down.

For example, in an early scene in the film, we view the security guard and his wife as they participate mechanically in their morning ritual. They get out of bed, attend to the baby, and heat the kettle on the stove. As the woman prepares to undress in the bathroom, we hear the sounds of her baby crying, and as her tired face reflected in the mirror begins to break into tears, the fragment abruptly cuts to black. This scene is immediately followed by a shot of the young Romanian boy eating food out of a bin located on the side of a busy road. As the passing cars draw to a halt, the boy looks over his shoulder, and we see a man and a woman in an expensive car staring at the boy in a dismissive way. Feeling uncomfortable, the boy walks away, the scene cuts to black and we are presented with another fragment, this one set in a university dorm where Maximilian and his roommate are participating in a conversation which we, however, enter mid-sentence. The discussion, we quickly learn, concerns a complicated puzzle that Maximilian is trying to crack and, as the roommate reveals the solution to his friend, the screen cuts to black, and to a new scene located in an orphanage.

*Figure 3: 71 Fragments of a Chronology of Chance.*

Like the puzzle that features in the film, *71 Fragments* has an intriguing, puzzle-like structure, though it is not a puzzle that can be readily solved. In keeping with the title *Code Unknown* (2000) (a film directed by Haneke which also deals with themes pertaining to war, migration, and strained relationships, and which is also highly fragmentary in its structure) the "code" for the seventy-one fragments that make up the film remains "unknown". "[M]y films", Haneke states, "pose certain questions, and it would be counterproductive if I were to answer these questions myself".[42] Rather, in keeping with Kluge's delineation of the task of *Autorenkino* – within which the role of the viewer is not to "understand" the intentions of the director but to actively participate in the film's construction[43] – what is crucial for

---

**42** | Sharrett, "The World That is Known: An Interview with Michael Haneke", p. 29.
**43** | Harmut Bitomsky, Harun Farocki and Klaus Henrichs, "Gespräch mit Alexander Kluge: Über *Die Patriotin*, Geschichte und Filmarbeit", *Filmkritik*, 275 (November, 1979), p. 510. Drawing on the example of the child at play as the model of his conception of an active, imaginative spectator, Kluge claims that just as the imagination of children is more readily stimulated by building blocks than by electrical train sets, so too is the imagination

Haneke is that the open, fragmentary form of the film facilitates the active, creative participation of the audience. "This", he notes,

is my principle concern after all: the film should not come to an end on the screen, but engage the spectators and find its place in their cognitive and emotional framework. In short, film as such does not exist, it comes to exist only in the minds of the spectators. [...] The author of the film puts markers and signposts into place; the spectators' potential for fantasy and emotion then unfolds between these markers.[44]

It is clear from this statement that Kluge's ideas have had an important impact on the development of Haneke's work, an influence most clearly manifested in Haneke's reference to the film in "the minds of the spectators": a phrase frequently employed by Kluge to describe the role that an experimental film practice can play in the establishment of an alternative public sphere within which viewers are encouraged to actively participate in the meaning-making process surrounding issues, policies, events, and ideas that impact on the world in which they live.[45] Haneke has certainly sought to achieve

---

of the spectator more effectively cultivated by films with the unfinished structure of a "construction site" or building in process. See Rainer Lewandowski, "Interview" in: *Die Filme von Alexander Kluge*, ed. Rainer Lewandowski, Hildesheim and New York: Olms Presse, 1980, p. 42. "I believe", Kluge states, "that it is [...] easier for the spectator to connect his experiences with a film that has breaks than with a perfect film. My editor always says: Weak films make strong viewers – strong films make weak viewers", to which Kluge adds: "a construction site is more advantageous than complete houses". See Jürgen Bevers, Klaus Kreimeier and Jutta Müller, "'Eine Baustelle ist vorteilhafter als ganze Häuser': Ein Gespräch mit Alexander Kluge", *Spuren: Zeitschrift für Kunst und Gesellschaft* I (Februar/März, 1980), p. 17.

44 | Haneke, "*71 Fragments of a Chronology of Chance:* Notes to the Film", p. 171.

45 | See, for example, Reitz, Kluge, and Reinke, "Word and Film", p. 87.

something similar through his portrayal of the shooting (and the events that preceded it) in *71 Fragments*. Instead of presenting the viewer with an informative "reading" of these events, the open, unfinished character of the film encourages the audience to draw on their own experience in an attempt to fill in the gaps between the fragments and, in doing so, to engage imaginatively with the material on screen.

It is not, however, just the fragmentary structure of the film which cultivates this active, imaginative mode of engagement. Rather, as touched on previously in relation to the scene that focuses on a telephone conversation between the man and his daughter, Haneke frequently makes use of long takes to stimulate the active, imaginative participation of the viewer. This emphasis on long takes is extremely important because it is by slowing down the pace that Haneke is able to cultivate a mode of engagement which differs significantly from the distant, "glacial" relationship fostered by television news programs; the latter of which (while also fragmentary in their structure) employ voiceover as a form of "glue" that both binds the fragments together[46] and irons out any ambiguities generated by the often eclectic collection of images on screen. Instead of packaging his stories in a manner that facilitates the rapid consumption of information, Haneke's extensive use of long takes encourages the audience to experience the image on screen; to inhabit the moment; and to feel the characters' pain, not through a process of identification, but by encouraging the audience to reflect on the kind of societal conditions that produce such alienation, loneliness, and despair.

---

**46** | This concept is taken from Siegfried Kracauer's analysis of the "glue" employed by "movie theatres" to transform films that are, in essence, fragmentary in their structure into "organic creations". See Siegfried Kracauer, "Cult of Distraction: On Berlin's Picture Palaces" in: *The Mass Ornament: Weimar Essays*, ed. Thomas Y. Levin, Cambridge, Mass. and London: Harvard University Press, 1995, p. 328.

For example, in an early scene in *71 Fragments*, we view Maximilian standing at the end of a table-tennis table hitting balls that are being fired at him (at a rapid, relentless pace) by a machine which is partly visible at the bottom of the screen. The image is dominated by grey, and we watch the student's automated gestures, examine his distressed face, and listen to the sound of the balls bouncing on the table for an uninterrupted period of nearly three minutes. What is powerful about this scene is the way in which one's relationship to and engagement with the image becomes more nuanced with both the repetition of his actions and the passing of time. As Haneke himself has pointed out in relation to this scene, instead of presenting the shot in the form of "information"[47] (a scenario in which we would only need to see the shot briefly to register that Maximilian is practicing his game), the extended presentation of the scene prompts us to think in depth about what it is that we are actually viewing, to feel the mechanical rhythm of Maximilian's actions, and to reflect on the source of the anxiety written across his face. This highly reflective mode of engagement is also cultivated later on in the film when we are presented with a fragmentary image of a monitor featuring video footage of Maximilian participating in a competitive game of table-tennis. The shot remains on the monitor, but as we hear the voice of his coach analysing the footage and aggressively chastising him for his mistakes, we feel the pressure and imagine the distressed, anxious look returning to Maximilian's face.

---

**47** | Serge Toubiana and Michael Haneke, "71 Fragments d'une Chronologie du Hasard: Entretien avec Michael Haneke par Serge Toubiana", DVD extra on Michael Haneke, *71 Fragments of a Chronology of Chance*, Madman Films (2007).

*Figure 4: 71 Fragments of a Chronology of Chance*

## Growing Wings

> [O]nly by virtue of the absolute negativity of collapse does art enunciate the unspeakable: utopia. In this image of collapse all the stigmata of the repulsive and loathsome in modern art gather. Through the irreconcilable renunciation of the semblance of reconciliation, art holds fast to the promise of reconciliation in the midst of the unreconciled: This is the true consciousness of an age in which the real possibility of utopia – that given the level of productive forces the earth could here and now be paradise – converges with the possibility of total catastrophe [...] as if art wanted to prevent the catastrophe by conjuring up its image.[48]
>
> THEODOR. W. ADORNO

---

**48** | Theodor W. Adorno, *Aesthetic Theory*, London and New York: Continuum, 1997, pp. 41-2.

The picture of *71 Fragments* sketched in this chapter is of a film that is disturbingly bleak. In addition to the acts of violence that take place at the end of the film, Haneke presents us with a series of characters whose lives are haunted by meaninglessness and whose relationships are marked, for the most part, by an absence of warmth, compassion, and human connection. In the news reports that intersperse the film, we learn that war, violence, terror and despair are an everyday part of the world in which we live; a world presented by television news programs in a manner that renders viewers numb to the suffering on screen.

Haneke, however, has stated that his "films are the expression of a desire for a better world"[49] and, although *71 Fragments* is very dark, it is far from nihilistic. "You should", Haneke states in a manner reminiscent of Adorno,

> always rebel against what's wrong. You can rebel against that in a film by showing it. But by showing it in a way that gives you a desire for an alternative, not in a way that makes it consumable.[50]

It is this emphasis on cultivating an active, imaginative mode of engagement that aligns Haneke's delineation of the possibilities of film with Kluge's analysis of the utopian promise of cinema. Although, as Haneke himself has pointed out, the world isn't as bleak (or, at least, as uniformly bleak) as the world presented in the trilogy[51], his approach not only "mobilises powers of resistance"[52] against the bleak, alienated image of life presented on screen but, in doing so, he encourages viewers to imagine how – and with what effects – life could, in reality, be transformed into something very different.

---

**49** | Toubiana and Haneke, "71 Fragments d'une Chronologie du Hasard: Entretien avec Michael Haneke par Serge Toubiana".
**50** | Ibid.
**51** | Assheuer and Haneke, *Nahaufnahme Michael Haneke. Gespräche mit Thomas Assheuer*, pp. 52-3.
**52** | Ibid., p. 133.

As Haneke notes in another context, the crucial point is to take the audience seriously and to "respect" their "capacity for perception and personal responsibility, that conceal in their gesture of refusal more utopia than all the bastions of representation and cheap consolation". It is only "[b]y leaving out the portrayal of happiness, [that] wishing", he writes, "grows wings".[53]

---

**53** | Michael Haneke, "Terror and Utopia of Form. Addicted to Truth. A Film Story about Robert Bresson's *Aus hazard Balthazar*" in: *Robert Bresson*, ed. James Quandt, Toronto: Toronto International Film Festival Group, 1998, pp. 558-9.

# References

Adorno, Theodor W., "On Popular Music" in: Richard Leppert, ed., *Essays on Music* Berkeley and Los Angeles: University of California Press, 2002.

Adorno, Theodor W., "Transparencies on Film" in: *The Culture Industry: Selected Essays on Mass Culture*, J.M. Bernstein ed., London and New York: Routledge, 2001.

Adorno, Theodor W., "The Schema of Mass Culture" in: *The Culture Industry: Selected Essays on Mass Culture*, ed. J.M. Bernstein, London and New York: Routledge, 2001.

Adorno, Theodor W., "How to Look at Television" in: *The Culture Industry: Selected Essays on Mass Culture*, ed. J.M. Bernstein, London and New York: Routledge, 2001.

Adorno, Theodor W., *Aesthetic Theory*, London and New York: Continuum, 1997.

Adorno, Theodor W., *Gesammelte Schriften*, vol. 3, ed. Rolf Tiedemann, Frankfurt am Main: Suhrkamp Verlag, 1997.

Adorno, Theodor W. and Walter Benjamin, *Briefwechsel: 1928-1940*, ed. Henri Lonitz, Frankfurt am Main: Suhrkamp, 1994.

Adorno, Theodor and Eisler, Hanns, *Composing for the Films*, London and Atlantic Highlands: The Athlone Press, 1994.

Adorno, Theodor W., "Transparencies on Film" in: *The Culture Industry: Selected Essays on Mass Culture*, London and New York: Routledge, 1991.

Adorno, Theodor W., "Arnold Schoenberg 1874-951" in *Prisms*, trans. Samuel and Shierry Weber, Cambridge, Mass.: The MIT Press, 1990.

Adorno, Theodor, "Commitment" in: Theodor Adorno, Walter Benjamin, Ernst Bloch, Bertolt Brecht and Georg Lukacs, *Aesthetics and Politics*, London and New York: Verso, 1990.

Adorno, Theodor, "Letters to Walter Benjamin" in: Theodor Adorno, Walter Benjamin, Ernst Bloch, Bertolt Brecht and Georg Lukacs, *Aesthetics and Politics*, London and New York: Verso, 1990.

Adorno, Theodor W., *Introduction to the Sociology of Music*, trans. E.B. Ashton, New York: Continuum, 1989.

Anonymous, "Merlin breaks silence on *Big Brother* protest", *Sydney Morning Herald* (14 June, 2004).

Anonymous, "Keine Wiener 'Konzentrationswoche'", *Die Presse* (7 June, 2000).

Arns, Inka and Sylvia Sasse, "Subversive Affirmation: On Mimesis as a Strategy of Resistance" in: *East Art Map: Contemporary Art and Eastern Europe*, ed. IRWIN, London: Afterall, 2006.

Art, David, *The Politics of the Nazi Past in Germany and Austria*, New York: Cambridge University Press, 2006.

Assheuer, Thomas and Michael Haneke, *Nahaufnahme Michael Haneke. Gespräche mit Thomas Assheuer*, Berlin: Alexander Verlag, 2008.

Benjamin, Walter, "The Work of Art in the Age of its Technological Reproducibility" in: Walter Benjamin, *Selected Writings: Volume 4, 1938-1940*, Cambridge, Mass. and London, England: Harvard University Press, 2003.

Benjamin, Walter, "Paralipomena to 'On the Concept of History'" in: Howard Eiland and Michael W. Jennings ed., *Walter Benjamin, Selected Writings: Volume 4, 1938-1940*, Cambridge, Mass. and London, England: Harvard University Press, 2003.

Benjamin, Walter, "Franz Kafka: On the Tenth Anniversary of His Death" in: *Walter Benjamin, Selected Writings: Volume 2*, ed. Michael W. Jennings, Howard Eiland and Gary Smith, Cambridge, Mass.: Harvard University Press, 1999.

Benjamin, Walter, "Some Motifs in Baudelaire" in: *Charles Baudelaire: A Lyric Poet in the Era of High Capitalism*, London and New York: Verso, 1997.

Benjamin, Walter, *The Arcades Project*, Cambridge, Mass., and London, England: Harvard University Press, 1999.

Benjamin, Walter, "The Handkerchief" in: *Selected Writings-Volume 2: 1927-1934*, Michael Jennings, Howard Eiland and Gary Smith, ed. Rodney Livingstone, Cambridge and London: The MIT Press, 1999.

Benjamin, Walter, "Central Park", in Walter Benjamin, *Selected Writings: Volume 4, 1938-1940*, Cambridge, Mass. and London, England: Harvard University Press, 2003.

Benjamin, Walter, "The Storyteller: Reflections on the Works of Nikolai Leskov" in: Walter Benjamin, *Illuminations*, ed. Hannah Arendt, London: Fontana Press, 1992.

Benjamin, Walter, *Gesammelte Schriften*, ed. Rolf Tiedemann and Hermann Schweppenhäuser, vol. 1.2, Frankfurt am Main: Suhrkamp, 1974.

Benzaquén, Adriana S., "Thought and Utopia in the Writings of Adorno, Horkheimer, and Benjamin", *Utopian Studies*, Vol. 9, No 2 (1998).

Beuys, Joseph, "Difesa della Natura: Discussion by/Discussione di Joseph Beuys" in: *Joseph Beuys: The Art of Cooking*, ed. Lucrezia De Domizio Durini, Milano: Edizioni Charta, 1999.

Bevers, Jürgen, Klaus Kreimeier und Jutta Müller, "'Eine Baustelle ist vorteilhafter als ganze Häuser': Ein Gespräch mit Alexander Kluge", *Spuren: Zeitschrift für Kunst und Gesellschaft* I, Februar/März, 1980.

Biesenbach, Klaus, Anna-Catharina Gebbers and Aino Laberenz ed., *Christoph Schlingensief*, Köln: Walther König, 2014.

Biltereyst, Daniel, "*Big Brother* and Its Moral Guardians: Reappraising the Role of Intellectuals in the *Big Brother* Panic" in: Ernest Mathijs and Janet Jones ed., *Big Brother International: Formats, Critics and Publics*, London and New York: Wallflower Press, 2004.

Bitomsky, Harmut, Harun Farocki, and Klaus Henrichs, "Gespräch mit Alexander Kluge: Über *Die Patriotin*, Geschichte und Filmarbeit", *Filmkritik*, 275 (November, 1979).

Bloch, Ernst and Theodor W. Adorno, "Something's Missing: A Discussion between Ernst Bloch and Theodor W. Adorno on the Contradictions of Utopian Longing" in: Ernst Bloch, *The Utopian Function of Art and Literature: Selected Essays*, Cambridge and London: The MIT Press, 1988.

Boehncke, Heiner and Alexander Kluge, "Die Rebellion des Stoffs gegen die Form und der Form gegen den Stoff: Der Protest als Erzähler" in: Heiner Boehncke, Johannes Beck and Klaus Bergmann ed., *Das B. Traven-Buch*, Reinbek bei Hamburg: Rowohlt, 1976.

Bogdan, Robert, *Freak Show: Presenting Human Oddities for Amusement and Pleasure*, Chicago: University of Chicago Press, 1988.

Boucher Geoff, *Adorno Reframed*, London: IB Tauris, 2013.

Brecht, Bertolt, "The Threepenny Lawsuit" in: Marc Silberman ed., *Bertolt Brecht on Film and Radio* (London: Methuen, 2001).

Brecht, Bertolt, "The Modern Theatre is the Epic Theatre" in: *Brecht on Theatre: The Development of an Aesthetic*, ed. John Willett, New York: Hill and Wang, 1998.

Bruck, Jan, "Brecht's and Kluge's Aesthetics of Realism", *Poetics*, No.17, 1988.

Buck-Morss, Susan, "Aesthetics and Anaesthetics: Walter Artwork Essay Reconsidered", *New Formations*, 20 (Summer, 1993).

Cook, Roger F., "Film Images and Reality: Alexander Kluge's Aesthetics of Cinema", *Colloquia Germanica*, 18, No. 4 (1985), pp. 281-299.

Cook, Deborah, *The Culture Industry Revisited: Theodor W. Adorno on Mass Culture* Lanham and London: Rowman & Littlefield, 1996.

Czernin, Hubertus ed., *Wofür ich mich meinetwegen entschuldige. Haider, beim Wort genommen*, Wien: Czernin Verlag, 2000.

Dawson, Jan, "'But Why are the Questions so Abstract?': An Interview with Alexander Kluge" in: *Alexander Kluge and the Occa-*

sional Work of a Female Slave, ed. Jan Dawson, New York: Zoetrope, 1977.
Dax, Max and Christoph Schlingensief, "Überwindung des Theaters", Spex, No. 328 (Sept/Okt, 2010).
Diedrichson, Diedrich, "Diskurverknappunsbekämpfung und negatives Gesamtkunstwerk: Christoph Schlingensief und seine Musik" in: Pia Janke and Teresa Kovacs ed., *Der Gesamtkünstler Christoph Schlingensief*, Wien: Praesens, 2011.
Diedrichson, Diedrich, "Magie und Massenarbeitslosigkeit, Christoph Schlingensiefs 'Chance 2000' im 'Prater' in Prenzlauer Berg" in: Alexander Wewerka ed., *Zeichen 4, Engagement und Skandal*, Berlin: Alexander Verlag, 2002.
Eder, Klaus and Peter Hamm, "Reise in der Wirklichkeit: Ein Gespräch mit Alexander Kluge und Volker Schlöndorff über das Projekt eines Krieg- und Frieden-Films," *Kirche und Film*, 3 (März, 1982).
Finke, Johannes and Matthias Wulff ed., *Chance 2000: Die Dokumenation. Phänomen, Materialien, Chronologie*, Berlin: Lautsprecher, 1999.
Forrest, Tara ed., *Alexander Kluge: Raw Materials For the Imagination*, Amsterdam: Amsterdam University Press, 2012.
Forrest, Tara and Anna Teresa Scheer ed., *Christoph Schlingensief: Art Without Borders* Bristol and Chicago: Intellect, 2010.
Gade, Solveig, "Putting the Public Sphere to the Test: On Publics and Counter-Publics in *Chance 2000*" in: *Christoph Schlingensief: Art Without Borders*, ed. Tara Forrest and Anna Teresa Scheer, Bristol and Chicago: Intellect, 2010.
Gade, Solveig, "Playing the Media Keyboard: The Political Potential of Performativity in Christoph Schlingensief's Electioneering Circus" in: Rune Gade and Anne Jerslev ed., *Performative Realism: Interdisciplinary Studies in Art and Media*, Copenhagen: Museum Tusculanum Press, 2005.
Gaensheimer, Susanne ed., *Christoph Schlingensief: Deutscher Pavillon 2011, 54. Internationale Kunstausstellung La Biennale Di Venezia*, Köln: Kiepenheuer & Witsch, 2011.

Gingrich, Andre, "A Man for All Seasons: An Anthropological Perspective on Public Representation and Cultural Politics of the Austrian Freedom Party" in: *The Haider Phenomenon in Austria*, ed. Wodak and Pelinka, New Brunswick and London: Transaction Publishers, 2002.

Grabner, Franz, "'Der Name der Erbsünde ist Verdrängung': Ein Gespräch mit Michael Haneke" in: Christian Wessely, Gerhard Larcher, and Franz Grabner ed., *Michael Haneke und seine Filme: Eine Pathologie der Konsumgesellschaft*, Marburg: Schüren Verlag, 2005.

Gregor, Ulrich, "Interview" in: *Herzog/Kluge/Straub* ed. by Peter W. Jansen and Wolfram Schütte, München and Wien: Carl Hanser Verlag, 1976.

Grissemann, Stefan and Michael Omasta, "Herr Haneke, wo bleibt das Positive?" in: Alexander Horwath ed., *Der Siebente Kontinent: Michael Haneke und seine Filme*, Wien and Zürich: Europaverlag, 1991.

Grundmann, Roy, ed., *A Companion to Michael Haneke*, Malden and Oxford: Wiley-Blackwell, 2010.

Haneke, Michael, "*71 Fragments of a Chronology of Chance*: Notes to the Film" in: Willy Riemer ed., *After Postmodernism: Austrian Literature and Film in Transition*, Riverside: Ariadne Press, 2000.

Haneke, Michael, "Terror and Utopia of Form. Addicted to Truth. A Film Story about Robert Bresson's *Aus hazard Balthazar*" in: James Quandt, ed., *Robert Bresson*, Toronto: Toronto International Film Festival Group, 1998.

Haneke, Michael, "Film als Katharis" in: Francesco Bono ed., *Austria (in)felix: zum österreichischen Film der 8oer Jahre*, Graz: Edition Blimp, 1992.

Harlan, Volker, *What is Art?: Conversation with Joseph Beuys*, Forest Row: Claireview, 2007.

Hansen, Miriam, "Alexander Kluge, Cinema and the Public Sphere: The Construction Site of Counter-History," *Discourse*, 6 (1983).

Harlan, Volker, "Conversation with Joseph Beuys" in: *What is Art?: Conversation with Joseph Beuys*, ed. Volker Harlan, Forest Row: Clairview Books, 2007.

Heineke, Thekla and Sandra Umathum ed., *Christoph Schlingensiefs Nazis Rein*, Frankfurt am Main: Suhrkamp, 2002.

Hopf, Florian, '"Feelings Can Move Mountains...': An Interview with Alexander Kluge on the Film *The Power of Feelings*" in: *Alexander Kluge: Raw Materials for the Imagination*, ed. Tara Forrest, Amsterdam: Amsterdam University Press, 2012.

Horkheimer, Max and Theodor W. Adorno, *Dialectic of Enlightenment: Philosophical Fragments*, Stanford: Stanford University Press, 2002.

Janke, Pia and Teresa Kovacs ed., *Der Gesamtkünstler Christoph Schlingensief*, Wien: Praesens, 2011.

Kaes, Anton, "In Search of Germany: Alexander Kluge's The Patriot" in: *Alexander Kluge: Raw Materials For the Imagination*, ed. Tara Forrest, Amsterdam: Amsterdam University Press, 2012.

Kluge, Alexandra and Rainer Frey, "Interview mit Alexander Kluge: Eine realistische Haltung müßte der Zuschauer haben, müßte ich haben, müßte der Film haben", *Filmfaust* 20 (November 1980).

Kluge, Alexandra and Bion Steinborn, "Film is das natürliche Tauschverhältnis der Arbeit...", *Filmfaust* 1.6 (December, 1977).

Kluge, Alexander, *Theorie der Erzählung: Frankfurter Poetikvorlesungen*, Berlin: Suhrkamp Verlag, 2013.

Kluge, Alexander, "The Political as Intensity of Everyday Feelings" in: *Alexander Kluge: Raw Materials For the Imagination*, ed. Tara Forrest, Amsterdam: Amsterdam University Press, 2013.

Kluge, Alexander, "On Film and the Public Sphere" in: Tara Forrest ed., *Alexander Kluge: Raw Materials For the Imagination*, Amsterdam: Amsterdam University Press, 2012.

Kluge, Alexander and Klaus Eder, "Debate on the Documentary Film: Conversation with Klaus Eder, 1980" in: *Alexander Kluge: Raw Materials For the Imagination*, ed. Tara Forrest, Amsterdam: Amsterdam University Press, 2012.

Kluge, Alexander, "The Sharpest Ideology: That Reality Appeals to its Realistic Character" in: *Alexander Kluge: Raw Materials For the Imagination*, ed. Tara Forrest, Amsterdam: Amsterdam University Press, 2012.

Kluge, Alexander, "Foreword" in: *Christoph Schlingensief: Art Without Borders*, ed. Tara Forrest and Anna Teresa Scheer, Bristol and Chicago: Intellect, 2010.

Kluge, Alexander and Christoph Schlingensief, "In erster Linie bin ich Filmemacher: Begegnung mit Christoph Schlingensief" in: *Alexander Kluge: Magazin des Glücks*, ed. Sebastian Huber and Claus Philipp, Wien: Springer-Verlag, 2007.

Kluge, Alexander, *The Devil's Blind Spot: Tales from the New Century*, trans. Martin Chalmers and Michael Hulse, New York: New Directions, 2004.

Kluge, Alexander, *Die Lücke, die der Teufel läßt: Im Umfeld des neuen Jahrhunderts*, Frankfurt am Main: Suhrkamp Verlag, 2003.

Kluge, Alexander and Christoph Schlingensief, "Ein Kaktus für Richard Wagner: Schlingensiefs *Ring des Nibelungen* in Africa" in: *Alexander Kluge, Facts & Fakes, Fernseh-Nachschriften 2/3: Herzblut trifft Kunstblut – Erster imaginärer Opernführer*, Christian Schulte and Reinald Gußmann, Berlin: Vorwerk 8, 2001.

Kluge, Alexander, "It is a mistake to Think that the Dead are Dead: Obituary for Heiner Müller" in: *The Power of Intellectuals in Contemporary Germany*, ed Michael Geyer, Chicago and London: University of Chicago Press, 2001.

Kluge, Alexander, "The Moment of Tragic Recognition with a Happy Ending" in: *The Power of Intellectuals in Contemporary Germany*, ed. Michael Geyer, Chicago and London: University of Chicago Press, 2001.

Kluge, Alexander and Christoph Schlingensief, "Freiheit für Alles, 1. Teil. Gespräch zwischen Alexander Kluge und Christoph Schlingensief"' in: *Schlingensiefs Ausländer Raus: Bitte Liebt Österreich*, ed. Matthias Lilienthal and Claus Philipp, Frankfurt am Main: Suhrkamp, 2000.

Kluge, Alexander and Christoph Schlingensief, "Freiheit für Alles, 2. Teil. Gespräch zwischen Alexander Kluge and Christoph Schlingensief" in: *Schlingensiefs Ausländer Raus: Bitte Liebt Österreich*, ed. Matthias Lilienthal and Claus Philipp, Frankfurt am Main: Suhrkamp, 2000.

Kluge, Alexander, "Interview von Ulrich Gregor (1976)" in: Alexander Kluge, *In Gefahr und größter Not bringt der Mittelweg den Tod: Texte zu Kino, Film, Politik*, ed. Christian Schulte, Berlin: Vorwerk 8, 1999.

Kluge, Alexander, "Ein Hauptansatz des Ulmer Instituts (1980)" in: Alexander Kluge, *In Gefahr und größter Not bringt der Mittelweg den Tod: Texte zu Kino, Film, Politik*, ed. Christian Schulte, Berlin: Vorwerk 8, 1999.

Kluge, Alexander, "Pact with a Dead Man" in: *West German Filmmakers on Film: Visions and Voices*, ed. Eric Rentschler, New York and London: Holmes & Meier, 1988.

Kluge, Alexander, *Die Macht der Gefühle*, Frankfurt am Main: Zweitausendeins, 1984.

Kluge, Alexander, "Text der Pressekonferenz mit Alexander Kluge über *Die Macht der Gefühle* in Venedig am 5. September 1983", *Kinemathek*, 20 (September, 1983).

Kluge, Alexander, ed., *Bestandsaufnahme: Utopie Film*, Frankfurt: Zweitausendeins, 1983.

Kluge, Alexander, *Die Patriotin: Texte/Bilder 1-6*, Frankfurt am Main: Zweitausendeins, 1979.

Kluge, Alexander, "Der Luftangriff auf Halberstadt am 8. April 1945" in: Alexander Kluge, *Neue Geschichten. Hefte 1-18: 'Unheimlichkeit der Zeit'*, Frankfurt am Main: Suhrkamp, 1978.

Kluge, Alexander, *Gelegenheitsarbeit einer Sklavin. Zur realistischen Methode*, Frankfurt: Suhrkamp Verlag, 1975.

Koch, Gertrud and Heide Schlüpmann, "'Nür Trümmern trau ich ...'. Ein Gespräch mit Alexander Kluge" in: *Kanalarbeit: Medienstrategien im Kulturwandel*, ed. Hans Ulrich Reck, Basel and Frankfurt am Main: Roter Stern, 1998.

Koch, Lars, "Christoph Schlingensiefs Bilderstörungsmaschine", *Zeitschrift für Literaturwissenschaft und Linguistik*, 44: 174 (2014).

Koegel, Alice and Kasper König ed., *AC: Christoph Schlingensief: Church of Fear*, Köln: Museum Ludwig and Verlag der Buchhandlung Walther König, 2005.

Koerner, Morgan, "Subversions of the Medical Gaze: Disability and Media Parody in Christoph Schlingensiefs *Freakstars 3000*" in: Gabrielle Mueller and James M. Skidmore eds., *Cinema and Social Change in Germany and Austria*, Waterloo: Wilfried Laurier Press, 2012.

Kötz Michael and Petra Höhne, *Sinnlichkeit des Zusammenhangs: Zur Filmarbeit von Alexander Kluge*, Köln: Prometh, 1981.

Kracauer, Siegfried, "Cult of Distraction: On Berlin's Picture Palaces" in: *The Mass Ornament: Weimar Essays*, ed. Thomas Y. Levin, Cambridge, Mass. and London: Harvard University Press, 1995.

Kümmel, Peter, "Der Mann mit der Moralkelle. "Ordnen Sie folgende KZ von Nord nach Süd": Christoph Schlingensief parodiert Günther Jauchs Rateshow", *Die Zeit*, No.13 (21 March, 2002): http://www.zeit.de/2002/13/200213_quiz3000_xml (Last viewed 9 July, 2014).

Langston, Richard, "Schlingensief's Peep-Show: Post-Cinematic Spectacles and the Public Space of History" in: Randall Halle and Reinhild Steingröver ed., *After the Avant-Garde: Contemporary German and Austrian Experimental Film*, New York: Camden House, 2008.

Lätzer, Stefan and Jakob Buhre, "Die Ursache liegt in der Zukunft", *Planet Interview*, 27 February, 2001: http://www.planet-interview.de/interviews/pi.php?interview=schlingensief-christoph (last accessed 8 July, 2014).

Lau, Miriam, "Der Dilettant als Medienphänomen – Über den Regisseur, Moderator und Hauptdarsteller Christoph Schlingensief", *Theaterheute*, No. 5 (May, 1998).

Laudenbach, Peter, "'Wir sind Glückssucher'", *Der Tagesspiegel*, 13.2.2012: http://www.tagesspiegel.de/kultur/wir-sind-gluecksucher/6201290.html (accessed 1 November 2013).

Laudenbach, Peter, '"Träume sind die Nahrung auf dem Weg zum Ziel,"' *brand eins: Wirtschaftsmagazin* 8 (2009).

Leupin, Rahel, "Grenzgänge zwischen Kunst und Politik: Joseph Beuys and Christoph Schlingensief" in: *Theater im Kasten: Rimini Protokoll, Castorfs Video, Beuys and Schlingensief, Lars von Trier*, ed. Andreas Kotte, Zürich: Chronos Verlag, 2007.

Lewandowski, Rainer, "Interview" in: *Die Filme von Alexander Kluge* ed. Rainer Lewandowski, Hildesheim and New York: Olms Presse, 1980.

Liebman, Stuart, "On New German Cinema, Art, Enlightenment, and the Public Sphere: An Interview with Alexander Kluge", *October* 46 (Fall, 1988).

Lilienthal, Matthias und Claus Philipp ed., *Schlingensiefs Ausländer Raus. Bitte Liebt Österreich*, Frankfurt am Main: Suhrkamp, 2000.

Lochte, Julia and Wilfried Schulz ed., *Schlingensief! Notruf für Deutschland. Über die Mission, das Theater und die Welt des Christoph Schlingensief*, Hamburg: Rotbuch Verlag, 1998.

Lutze, Peter C., *Alexander Kluge: The Last Modernist*, Detroit: Wayne State University Press, 1998.

Manoschek, Walter, "FPÖ, ÖVP, and Austria's Nazi Past" in: *The Haider Phenomenon in Austria*, ed. Ruth Wodak and Anton Pelinka, New Brunswick and London: Transaction Publishers, 2002.

Mesch, Claudia and Viola Michely ed., *Joseph Beuys: The Reader*, Cambridge, MA: Harvard University Press, 2007.

Claudia Mesch, "Institutionalizing Social Sculpture: Beuys' *Office for Direct Democracy through Referendum* Installation, 1972" in: Claudia Mesch and Viola Michely ed., *Joseph Beuys: The Reader*, Cambridge, MA.: The MIT Press, 2007.

Mießgang, Thomas, "Im Land der Lächler. Über Jelinek, Wuttke und Schlingensif, über Salzgurken und Sachertorten: Sittenbilder aus dem Künstlerkamp gegen die neue Regierung in Wien", *Die Zeit* (29 June, 2000).

Moeller, Hans-Bernard and George Lellis, *Volker Schlöndorff's Cinema: Adaption, Politics, and the 'Movie-Appropriate'*, Carbondale and Edwardsville: Southern Illinois University Press, 2002.

Musner, Lutz, "Memory and Globalization: Austria's Recycling of the Nazi Past and its European Echoes", *New German Critique*, No. 80 (Spring-Summer 2000).

Negt, Oskar and Alexander Kluge, *Public Sphere and Experience: Toward an Analysis of the Bourgeois and Proletarian Public Sphere*, Minneapolis and London: University of Minnesota Press, 1993.

Pavsek, Christopher, *The Utopia of Film: Cinema and Its Futures in Godard, Kluge, and Tahimik*, New York: Columbia University Press, 2013.

Phillip, Claus, "Vertrauenswürdige Irrtümer: Ein Gespräch mit Alexander Kluge", *Kolik*, 13 (2000).

Plato, *The Republic*, London: Penguin, 1987.

Poore, Carol, *Disability in Twentieth Century German Culture*, Ann Arbor: University of Michigan Press, 2007.

Puig, Claudia, "Elegant 'White Ribbon' gets all tied up in monotonous gloom", *USA Today* (January 8, 2010).

Rack, Jochen, "Gespräch mit Alexander Kluge: Wir Leben doch nicht nur in einer Gegenwart", *Sinn und Form*, 60.4 (2008).

Rajesh, Monisha, "Michael Haneke's Film Noir", *Time* (November 30, 2009).

Reitz, Edgar, Alexander Kluge and Wilfried Reinke, "Word and Film," *October* 46 (Fall, 1988).

Roberts, David, "Alexander Kluge and German History: 'The Air Raid on Halberstadt on 8.4.1945'" in: *Alexander Kluge: Raw Materials For the Imagination*, ed. Tara Forrest, Amsterdam: Amsterdam University Press, 2012.

Rötzer, Florian, "Kino und Grabkammer: Gespräch mit Alexander Kluge," in: *Die Schrift an der Wand: Alexander Kluge: Rohstoffe und Materialien*, ed. Christian Schulte, Osnabrück: Universitätsverlag Rasch, 2000.

Sacks, Shelly, "Seeing the phenomenon and imaginal thought: Trajectories for transformation in the work of Joseph Beuys and

Rudolf Steiner" in: *Joseph Beuys and Rudolf Steiner: Imagination, Inspiration, Intuition*, ed. Alison Holland, Melbourne: National Gallery of Victoria, 2007.

Sacks, Shelly, "Foreword" in: *What is Art? Conversation with Joseph Beuys*, ed. Volker Harlan, Forest Row: Claireville, 2004.

Schlingensief, Christoph, *Ich weiß, ich war's*, ed. Aino Laberenz, Köln: Kiepenheuer & Witsch, 2012.

Schlingensief, Christoph, *So schön wie hier kanns im Himmel gar nicht sein: Tagebuch einer Krebserkrankung*, Köln: Kiepenheur & Witsch, 2009.

Schlingensief, Christoph, "My work always has something to do with a change of perspective" (interviewed by Hans Ulrich Obrist) in: *AC: Christoph Schlingensief – Church of Fear*, ed. A. Koegel and K. König, Köln: Museum Ludwig and Walther König, 2005.

Schlingensief, Christoph, "*Kunst und Gemüse: Eine Erklärung*" in: *Theater ALS Krankheit*, ed. Carl Hegemann, Berlin: Alexander Verlag, 2004.

Schlingensief, Christoph, "Wir sind zwar nicht gut, aber wir sind da" in: *Schlingensief! Notruf für Deutschland. Über die Mission, das Theater und die Welt des Christoph Schlingensief*, ed. Julia Lochte and Wilfried Schulz, Hamburg: Rotbuch Verlag, 1998.

Scholem, Gershom and Theodor W. Adorno ed., *The Correspondence of Walter Benjamin: 1910-1940*, Chicago and London: The University of Chicago Press, 1994.

Schönherr, Ulrich, "Adorno and Jazz: Reflections on a Failed Encounter", *Telos*, No.87 (Spring, 1991).

Schulte, Christian ed., *Die Frage des Zusammenhangs: Alexander Kluge im Kontext*, Berlin: Vorwerk 8, 2012.

Schulte, Christian and Rainer Stollman ed., *Der Maulwurf kennt kein System: Beitrage zur gemeinsamen Philosophie von Oskar Negt und Alexander Kluge*, Bielefeld: transcript, 2005.

Schulte, Christian and Winfried Siebers ed., *Kluges Fernsehen: Alexander Kluges Kulturmagazine*, Frankfurt: Suhrkamp, 2002.

Schulte, Christian ed., *Die Schrift an der Wand. Alexander Kluge: Rohstoffe und Materialien*, Osnabrück: Universitätsverlag Rasch, 2000.

Schulte, Christian, ed., *Alexander Kluge: In Gefahr und größter Not bringt der Mittelweg den Tod. Texte zu Kino, Film, Politik*, Berlin: Vorwerk 8, 1999.

Sharrett, Christopher, "The World That is Known: An Interview with Michael Haneke", *Cineaste* (Summer, 2003).

Sombroek, Andreas, *Eine Poetik des Dazwischen: Zur Intermedialität und Intertextualität bei Alexander Kluge*, Bielefeld: transcript, 2005.

Steinborn, Bion, "'Unser Herrgott ist der erste Kernaggressor': Ein Gespräch mit Alexander Kluge und Volker Schlöndorff über (den Film) 'Krieg und Frieden'", *Filmfaust*, 32 (Februar-März, 1983).

Stoehr, Kevin L., "Haneke's Secession: Perspectivism and Anti-Nihilism in *Code Unknown* and *Caché*" in: *A Companion to Michael Haneke*, ed. Roy Grundmann, Malden and Oxford: Wiley Blackwell, 2010.

Stollmann, Rainer, "Nicht Alles, was einen in Wallung bringt, ist ein Gefühl: Gespräch mit Alexander Kluge" in: *Die Frage des Zusammenhangs: Alexander Kluge im Kontext*, ed. Christian Schulte, Berlin, Verlag Vorwerk 8 (2012).

Stollmann, Rainer, *Alexander Kluge: Zur Einführung*, Hamburg: Junius Verlag, 1998.

Tindemans, Klaes, "The Wounded German Body of Christoph Schlingensief" in: Lieven De Cauter, Rube De Roo and Karel Vanhaesebrouck ed., *Art and Activism in the Age of Globalization*, Rotterdam: NAi, 2011.

Uecker, Matthias, *Anti-Fernsehen? Alexander Kluge's* Fernsehproduktionen, Marburg: Schüren Verlag, 2000.

Uecker, Matthias, "'Für Kultur ist es nie zu spät!' – Alexander Kluge's Television Productions" in: Arthur Williams, Stuart Parkes, and Julian Preece ed., *'Whose Story?' – Continuities in Contemporary German-language Literature*, Bern: Peter Lang, 1998.

van der Horst, Jörg, "'So what was the actual truth? How did it all fit together?': Schlingensief, the Media and the Schlingensief Media" in: *Christoph Schlingensief*, Klaus Biesenbach, Anna-Catharina Gebbers, Aino Laberenz, Susanne Pfeffer ed., London, Koenig Books, 2013.

van Zoonen, Liesbet, "Desire and Resistance: *Big Brother in the Dutch Public Sphere*" in: *Big Brother International: Formats, Critics and Publics*, Ernest Mathijs and Janet Jones ed., London and New York: Wallflower Press, 2004.

Varney, Denise, "'Right Now Austria Looks Ridiculous'": *Please Love Austria!* – Reforging the Interaction Between Art and Politics" in: *Christoph Schlingensief: Art Without Borders*, Tara Forrest and Anna Teresa Scheer ed., Bristol and Chicago: Intellect, 2010.

Vogel, Amos, "Of Nonexisting Continents: The Cinema of Michael Haneke", *Film Comment*, Vol. 32, No. 4 (July/August, 1996).

von Moltke, Johannes, "Confusion of Feelings: Alexander Kluge on War, Film, and Emotion" in: *Screening the War: Perspectives on German Suffering*, Paul Cooke and Marc Silberman ed., Rochester: Camden House, 2010.

Wheatley, Catherine, *Michael Haneke's Cinema: The Ethic of the Image*, New York: Berghahn Books, 2009.

Wodak, Ruth and Anton Pelinka, "Introduction" in: Ruth Wodak and Anton Pelinka ed., *The Haider Phenomenon in Austria*, New Brunswick and London: Transaction Publishers, 2002.

Wood, Robin, "Hidden in plain sight: Robin Wood on Michael Haneke's Cache", *Artforum International*, Vol. 44, No. 5 (January, 2006).

## OTHER WORKS CITED

Haneke, Michael, *Code Unknown* (2000)
Haneke, Michael, *71 Fragments of a Chronology of Chance* (1994).
Kablitz-Post, Cordula, *Christoph Schlingensief. Die Piloten* (2009).
Kablitz-Post, Cordula, *Talk 2000* (2009).

Kluge, Alexander, *Theorie der Erzählung. Frankfurter Poetikvorlesungen* (2013).

Kluge, Alexander, "Die rechte Hand Gottes: Michael Haneke über seinen preisgekrönten Film *Das Weisse Band*", *News & Stories* (November 1, 2009).

Kluge, Alexander, "Was heißt 'guter Wille'?", Alexander Kluge, *Die poetische Kraft der Theorie & Alle Gefühle glauben an einen glücklichen Ausgang*, Edition filmmuseum 34, (2009).

Kluge, Alexander, *Die poetische Kraft der Theorie & Alle Gefühle glauben an einen glücklichen Ausgang*, Vol. 34, Edition filmmuseum (2009).

Kluge, Alexander, "Das Halten von Totenschädeln liegt mir nicht!", Alexander Kluge, *Freiheit für die Konsonanten! & Grenzfälle der Schadensregulierung*, Edition filmmuseum 32 (2008).

Kluge, Alexander, "Das Phänomen der Oper", Alexander Kluge, *Das Kraftwerk der Gefühle & Finsterlinge singen Bass*, Edition filmmuseum 33 (2008).

Kluge, Alexander, "Zauberwelt der Evolution", Alexander Kluge, *Krieg ist das Ende aller Pläne & Woher wir kommen, wohin wir gehen*, Edition filmmuseum 31 (2008).

Kluge, Alexander, "Das Weichziel ist der Mensch" (2008), *Freiheit für die Konsonanten! & Grenzfälle der* Schadensregulierung, Edition filmmuseum 32, (2008).

Kluge, Alexander, "Abschied von der sicheren Seite des Lebens" (A Farewell to the Secure Side of Life") (2002), Alexander Kluge, *Im Rausch der Arbeit & Abschied von der sicheren Seite des Lebens*, Edition filmmuseum 29, (2008).

Kluge, Alexander, "Die Guillotine oder die Kategorie der Plötzlichkeit", Alexander Kluge, Alexander Kluge, *Der Eiffelturm, King Kong und die weiße Frau & Mann ohne Kopf*, Edition filmmuseum 28, (2008).

Kluge, Alexander, "Der Wind, der reinigt das – " ("The Wind Will Clean it Off") (1996), Alexander Kluge, *Im Rausch der Arbeit & Abschied von der sicheren Seite des Lebens* (2008).

Kluge, Alexander, "Das Quietschen der Macht, wenn sie die Bremsen zieht", Alexander Kluge, *Freiheit für die Konsonanten! & Grenzfälle der Schadensregulierung*, Edition filmmuseum 32, (2008).

Kluge, Alexander, "Das Halten von Totenschädeln liegt mir nicht!" on the DVD: Alexander Kluge, *Freiheit für die Konsonanten! & Grenzfälle der Schadensregulierung* (2008) and "Das Phänomen der Oper" on the DVD: Alexander Kluge, *Das Kraftwerk der Gefühle & Finsterlinge singen Bass* (2008).

Kluge, Alexander, "Am Kältesten Punkt des Kalten Kriegs/Stephan Aust über ein Beispiel des Rüstungs-Wahns", *Primetime/Spätausgabe*, RTL, 29 October, 2006.

Kluge, Alexander, "Tür an Tür mit einem anderen Leben" (Radio Interview), *Das Blaue Sofa* (2006).

Kluge, Alexander, "Am Kältesten Punkt des Kalten Kriegs/Stephan Aust über ein Beispiel des Rüstungs-Wahns", *Primetime/Spätausgabe*, RTL, 29 October, 2006.

Kluge, Alexander, „Die Kirche der Angst/Erste attaistische Nachrichten von Christoph Schlingensief", *News & Stories*, SAT 1 (24 August, 2003).

Kluge, Alexander, "Theater der Handgreiflichkeit/Christoph Schlingensiefs Wiener Container", *News and Stories*, SAT 1, October 22, 2000.

Kluge, Alexander, "Theater der Handgreiflichkeit/Christoph Schlingensiefs Wiener Container", *News and Stories*, SAT 1, October 22, 2000.

Kluge, Alexander, Volker Schlöndorff, Stefan Aust, Axel Engstfeld (1982).

Kluge, Alexander, *Die Patriotin* (1979).

Poet, Paul, *Ausländer Raus. Schlingensiefs Container* (2005).

Schlingensief, Christoph, *Freakstars 3000* (2003).

Schlingensief, Christoph, *Quiz 3000: Du Bist die Katrastrophe* (2002)

Schlingensief, Christoph, *U 3000* (2000).

Schlingensief, Christoph, *Talk 2000* (1997).

Toubiana, Serge and Michael Haneke, "71 Fragments d'une Chronologie du Hasard: Entretien avec Michael Haneke par Serge Toubiana", DVD extra on Haneke, M. *71 Fragments of a Chronology of Chance*, Madman Films, 2007.

Wittlich, Angelika, *Alle Gefühle glauben an einer glücklichen Ausgang* (2002).

Printed by Printforce, United Kingdom